Extraordinary CAKES

Tom—
Cheers to
many years of
extraordinary
Baking

Extraordinary CAKES

RECIPES FOR BOLD AND SOPHISTICATED DESSERTS

KAREN KRASNE

Chef and Owner of Extraordinary Desserts

Written with Christina Wright
Photographs by Ray Kachatorian

RIZZOLI
NEW YORK

To my grandmother, Clara;
my mother, Sally;
and my daughter, Sahara.

First published in the United States of America in 2011
by Rizzoli International Publications, Inc.
300 Park Avenue South
New York, NY 10010
www.rizzoliusa.com

© 2011 Karen Krasne
All photographs © 2011 Ray Kachatorian

2018 2019 2020 / 10 9 8 7 6 5

Design by Lynne Yeamans
Printed in China

ISBN: 978-0-8478-5808-8

Library of Congress Control Number: 2011927160

Contents

Preface ✦ 6

Introduction ✦ 7

Preface

To me, a luscious and lovely cake celebrates all the good things in life. That's why everywhere I go, no matter where I go, I seem to carry one along with me. Whether I'm on my way to a party or to Paris, I have a carefully boxed, extraordinarily beautiful cake dangling by a ribbon from the fingers of one hand. I guess you could say that cake has become my calling card as well as my calling.

It's a passion that started in France, where I learned to cook and bake, and was nourished by years working as a pastry chef in kitchens in Europe and Mexico. (Those years of travel also developed my taste for combining exotic and far-flung flavors in my cake creations.) But my growing interest in—and total love for—pastry didn't find its full expression until I returned to San Diego in the late 1980s and set up a workspace (my dad's garage, actually) in which to develop my very own line of cakes. The positive response from restaurants, department store cafés, and individuals was all the encouragement I needed to open Extraordinary Desserts, a dessert café that I conceived of as a showroom for my cakes. It was 1988, and the café had a mere ten seats.

In the subsequent twenty-plus years, it has expanded to keep pace with my growing roster of cakes and a loyal clientele who even gladly stand in line when necessary. In 2004, I opened the second branch of Extraordinary Desserts in the Little Italy neighborhood of San Diego. A bakery restaurant with 175 seats, this new space was designed to feature a Zen-inspired décor. The *San Diego Union-Tribune* called it "the Bulgari of coffee houses." This suited me fine, since to this baker's eyes, some of the cakes glowing in the display cases are just as beautiful as jewels.

I've been amazingly fortunate to work in a community that enthusiastically embraces my passion for my craft. From day one, I created a signature style that calls for decorating cakes and other desserts with lavish garnishes of flowers, fine imported ribbons, and glittering splashes of edible gold leaf. By Extraordinary Desserts' twentieth anniversary, the staff had grown to more than a hundred, but I never relinquished my role as a hands-on baker and creator, and I continue to develop new cakes and desserts daily. I love to travel, and wherever I go, I explore desserts that are new to me and then incorporate their tastiest features into new recipes that I hope will continue to delight my customers.

It's a privilege to craft cakes for some of the most important and memorable moments in peoples' lives. Working with a couple to design a customized wedding cake that expresses their love for one another is inspiring, as is hearing "Happy Birthday" being sung in my restaurants, which happens very often. I truly love that my cakes and desserts often are integral to the most special occasions. Cakes have the magic of creating happiness. Bringing such joy to others is extremely gratifying to me, and a sweet reward for the many years I have spent learning to build extraordinary desserts.

—KAREN KRASNE

Introduction

I like to create cakes that contain complex textural differences and an element of surprise.

In keeping with this philosophy, most of the cakes in this book have multiple layers and many components. Because of this, I strongly recommend that you read through whichever recipe you are contemplating before diving right in. These are not cakes that you can bake, decorate, and eat in the same day.

That said, they are very manageable if you have a game plan and a little patience. In each recipe, I have listed the components in the order in which they will be used in assembling the finished cake creation. When you set out to make one of these cakes, I would advise you to create a personal cake plan, outlining the order in which you will make each component, based on which components can be prepared ahead of time and held until ready to use. Depending on how you break down your plan, you can prepare the components and assemble the cake over a time span of one to four days. Here is what a typical four-day cake plan might look like:

DAY 1: Bake the cake layer, make the simple syrup, and make the ganache.

DAY 2: Make the mousse, reheat the ganache, and assemble and freeze the cake.

DAY 3: Unmold the cake, frost the cake, decorate, and let thaw (often overnight).

DAY 4: Serve for dessert.

What follows is a listing of equipment and ingredients you will need to have and techniques you will need to be familiar with to make the cakes in this book. The more experienced a cake maker you are, the more comfortable you will be with adapting these to your own needs and tastes.

Unless otherwise specified, you will need the tools and baking equipment listed below, most of which are fairly standard. Some of the more specialized items can be easily found online or in your local craft or cake decorating supply store.

- **DRY AND WET MEASURING CUPS** help to ensure that ingredients are measured precisely. I like to use stainless-steel measuring cups for the dry ingredients because they are easy to clean and do not absorb odors or flavors. Clear glass liquid measuring cups are great for both hot and cold liquids, and allow you to see through the glass to get the most accurate measure. I always try to have several different sizes of liquid measuring cups on hand when I bake, ranging from as small as a ⅛-cup measure all the way to 2 cups.

- **HEATPROOF RUBBER SPATULAS AND WOODEN SPOONS** are useful for mixing, folding, and stirring cooked components such as custards and caramels. Offset spatulas are great for spreading pastry creams, whipped cream, curds, meringues, mousse, and frosting. Long, straight spatulas are needed to cleanly cover cakes with ganache or glaze. It is important for the straight spatula to be heavy-handled and not flexible. I like mine to be at least 2 inches longer than the diameter of the cake I am decorating.

- **A LONG SERRATED KNIFE** is key to slicing a baked cake into even layers. Most cakes in this book are 10 inches in diameter, so choose a knife that is 14 inches or longer. It will enable you to see both ends of the knife as you horizontally cut through the cake, ensuring that you are keeping the knife level and therefore cutting flat and even cake layers.

- **A PASTRY BRUSH** does not need to be fancy, just sturdy enough that it does not lose its bristles as you brush it across a cake layer. I prefer brushes that are 1 to 2 inches wide. Remember to thoroughly wash and dry pastry brushes after each use or the bristles will become sticky and harden.

- **PASTRY BAGS** are ideal not just for decorating a cake, but for piping creams, meringues, and mousse on top of cake layers during the assembly process to ensure even layers and an unexpected decorative touch. Disposable pastry bags save time in washing and are available online.

- **SIFTERS AND STRAINERS** come in many varieties and sizes. I like medium-gauge wire-mesh strainers that can be used alternately to strain wet liquids and to sift dry ingredients. Fine wire-mesh strainers are handy for dusting finished cakes with powdered sugar or cocoa powder. Two sizes will work for almost every cake I make: a medium-size one, no more than 8 inches in diameter, and a small one that performs double duty as a tea strainer.

- **NONREACTIVE, HEAVY SAUCEPANS** are essential when cooking delicate or temperamental fillings and sauces on the stovetop. They prevent pastry creams or curds from scorching and sugar from cooking unevenly or too quickly. This is especially true when cooking on an electric stovetop, where the heat is harder to control and maintain. Stainless steel, glass, and enamelware are three primary types of nonreactive cookware surfaces; they ensure that any acids you're using will not react with the cookware and create any off colors or tastes.

- **SILPATS** are washable, reusable silicone mats that are able to withstand high temperatures and can be used in place of parchment paper to line baking sheets when pouring out high-temperature items such as hot caramel or pralines. They function similarly to silicone baking molds in that they are flexible and do not need to be greased before use.

- **CANDY THERMOMETERS** are imperative for a novice baker, but experienced cooks can also benefit from their precision. Candy thermometers are available in several styles, from those enclosed only in glass to ones surrounded by stainless steel, and will ensure that your sugar or caramel is cooked to exactness. Remember to always cool candy thermometers upright, and test them in boiling water every so often to ensure that they are still reading true to temperature.

- **STAND MIXERS** are one of the most useful tools in any kitchen. From whipping egg whites to mixing dough, this machine has simplified the lives of pastry chefs and home bakers. I would strongly recommend having a least two sets of bowls and attachments for your stand mixer. This will alleviate the need to wash dishes in between steps in many of the processes in these recipes.

- **BLENDERS AND FOOD PROCESSORS** are incredibly helpful multi-use appliances. Blenders are great for thoroughly and easily emulsifying a mixture such as a ganache. Immersion blenders are handy in that you place the blender into the mixture instead of the other way around, whereas stand blenders generally offer more speeds. Food processors can grind nuts, turn out beautifully emulsified ganaches, and also puree fruits for sauces more easily than a stand blender; they also hold more volume.

- **CAKE PANS WITH REMOVABLE BOTTOMS** are used in almost all of the recipes in this book and can easily be found online. A cake pan with a removable bottom functions similarly to a springform pan in that the side and the bottom are

CLOCKWISE FROM TOP LEFT: SPRINGFORM ANGEL FOOD CAKE PAN, ROUND PAN WITH REMOVABLE BOTTOM, RECTANGULAR PAN, INDIVIDUAL CAVITY BUNDT PAN, PAPER BAKING RING MOLD, INDIVIDUAL SPRINGFORM PANS, INDIVIDUAL BAKING CUPS, SILICONE SQUARE SAVARIN MOLD, DOME MOLD, SQUARE PANS.

separate pieces, allowing for easier removal of the baked cake. *But they are not interchangeable:* In a pan with a removable bottom, the bottom lifts up and out of the pan. In a springform pan, the sides click in place inside a groove along the edge of the bottom of the pan. For the purposes of the cakes in this book, a cake pan with a removable bottom holds more volume. Therefore, using a springform pan in place of the one called for will affect the layering of the cake in the assembly process, and you will have small amounts of leftover creams, curds, or mousse during the assembly process.

- **OVEN THERMOMETERS** are invaluable to home bakers, as most home ovens have hot spots or tend to bake slightly higher or lower than the tempera-ture to which they are set. Oven thermometers hang from a clip inside the oven and will help guide you if your home oven is baking too hot or under temperature. I like to move my oven ther-mometer to different spots each time I bake to see if my oven has hot spots. I would also recommend that you check your cake for doneness approxi-mately three-quarters of the way into the estimated baking time, due to temperature fluctuations and differences in home ovens.

• A WIRE COOLING RACK speeds up the cooling process for a baked item by allowing air to circu-late all around it. Any shape or size will work, as long as the rack has feet that allow it to sit higher than the surface on which it is placed.

• WHEN ASSEMBLING THE CAKES IN THIS BOOK, YOU WILL NEED A FEW OTHER SMALL ITEMS: cardboard cake rounds and squares on which to place the bottom layer of the cake; assorted sizes and styles of pastry decorating tips, which can be purchased in sets or individually in any cake supply store or most craft stores; and parchment paper in sheets and rounds. A cake leveler and a revolving cake stand are strictly optional, though helpful if your budget allows; the former will make it easier to cut even cake layers, while the latter will simplify frosting an assembled cake. A cake divider allows you to mark individual slices precisely.

INGREDIENTS

The building blocks of even the most elaborate cakes are pretty basic: sugar, flour, eggs, and butter. Besides these, I occasionally call for slightly more exotic or less familiar ingredients, and have included where to find them in the Sources section of this book (page 171).

Some bakers are very particular about product brands, the color of the eggs they use, and whether or not to use only organic ingredients. Instead of limiting yourself in that manner, I encourage you to simply buy the best quality ingredients that you are able to, especially when a given ingredient will be featured prominently in your cake.

Just as important as having the right ingredi-ents is using them at the right temperature. When baking, a good rule of thumb is to bring all the ingredients to room temperature before using them. This is especially important for items such as eggs, butter (unless the recipe specifies cold butter), sour cream, cream cheese, and mascarpone—items that you would store in the refrigerator until using. The ingredients will blend together better when they are at the same temperature, which in turn creates smoother batters and yields a better end product. Planning ahead and making a cake plan will allow you to set all your ingredients aside with enough time to ensure they are all at the same temperature when you are ready to start mixing and baking.

Follow the guidelines below when selecting your ingredients.

• BUTTER: Always use unsalted butter at room temperature unless otherwise specified. For best results, try to find butter that has an average butterfat content of about 80 percent, such as Plugra. The

CLOCKWISE FROM TOP LEFT: FROZEN FRUIT PUREES, YUZU JUICE, FROZEN FRUIT CONCENTRATE, TRABLIT COFFEE EXTRACT, ROSE SYRUP, VANILLA EXTRACT, ALMOND FLOUR, CHOCOLATE CIGARETTES, MATCHA TEA, CHOCOLATE FLAKES, COCOA POWDER, ROSE PETALS, WHITE CHOCOLATE, GELATIN SHEETS, DARK CHOCOLATE, VARIOUS SORTS OF DRIED COCONUT.

lower the fat content, the more water the butter contains, which may adversely affect the outcome of the recipe.

- CHOCOLATE: When chocolate is the predominant flavor in a recipe, you may want to choose one with a strong enough flavor profile to stand up to being diluted by eggs, sugar, flour, and other ingredients. If the chocolate is playing a secondary role, a good choice might be a well-balanced blend of less intense beans. Always taste chocolate before deciding which kind to use in a recipe. I most often use Valrhona in my recipes because I prefer its characteristic strong notes and slight acidity.

- COCOA POWDER: I always use the alkalized variety, which has a rounder taste, and I am partial to the Valrhona brand, as it has a rich and deep flavor with a beautiful red mahogany color.

- EGGS: Unless otherwise specified, use large eggs in all recipes. Whether you choose brown or white, store-bought or fresh from the farm, is up to you.

- GELATIN: I insist on using gelatin sheets instead of the powdered variety. Powdered gelatin requires water in order to bloom and liquefy, which adds unnecessary liquid to the recipe. All of the recipes in this book that call for gelatin were tested using gold-strength gelatin sheets.

- GLUCOSE: Glucose is a liquid sweetener that discourages crystallization and ensures a silky texture. You can buy glucose from specialty suppliers (see Sources, page 171). Light corn syrup is an easy substitute.

- HEAVY CREAM: This is the exception to the room-temperature rule when it is being used for whipped cream. In this application, heavy cream should be kept refrigerated until ready to use or it will not whip up properly.

- HONEY: Stick to mild floral or fruit varieties. I like to support local beekeepers, but all natural supermarket brands will work just as well.

- NUTS: I prefer to leave the skin on nuts, as it enhances their flavor. Nuts should be purchased as close to the day of use as possible and stored in the refrigerator or freezer to delay them from turning rancid.

Now that you have your equipment and ingredients ready to go, it's time to actually make a cake. Whether you are a novice cake maker or an avid home baker, take another minute to once again read through the recipe and review your cake plan. While most of these recipes are not difficult to make, there are a lot of different parts, so being organized about which components of the recipe to make first will help you succeed.

Next, read through the essential techniques below. You'll use most of them when making the cakes in this book, so I've compiled them here for easy reference.

- **SCRAPING A VANILLA BEAN:** Using a small paring knife, slice the vanilla bean in half lengthwise. With the back of the knife (not the blade side) scrape the vanilla seeds from the bean. The seeds and the scraped bean itself can then be added to heating liquids to infuse flavor. Remove the bean before incorporating the infused liquid into a recipe. The soaked vanilla bean can then be rinsed, dried, and ground up with sugar to create vanilla-flavored sugar.

PROPER COLOR AND TEXTURE OF PRALINES COOLING ON A SILPAT

- **TOASTING NUTS:** Preheat the oven to 300°F. Place the nuts in a single layer on a baking sheet and bake in the center of the oven until lightly browned and fragrant. This should take between 10 and 15 minutes, depending on the quantity of nuts being toasted. Remove the nuts from the oven and allow to cool completely before using. To test for doneness, cut one nut in half: the center should be almost as lightly browned as the outside.

- **UNMOLDING THE BAKED CAKE:** Once the cake has completely cooled, it should release easily from its pan. You may need to gently run the blade of a metal spatula around the inside of the pan to fully separate the side of the cake from the side of the pan. Next, gently lift off the sides of the cake pan. To remove the bottom, place a parchment paper round on top of the cake and cover with a cardboard cake board. Flip the cake over onto the cake board so that it is now bottom side up. Gently pull the bottom of the cake pan off the cake. If it does not release easily, gently insert the tip of a paring knife in between the cake and the cake pan and lift slightly to separate the "seal" that may have been created as the cake baked. You should then be able to easily lift off the bottom of the pan.

- **REHEATING GANACHE OR CARAMEL:** Ganache or caramel that has been made in advance and stored in the refrigerator will need to be reheated to the proper consistency called for in the recipe before using. If stored in the refrigerator, allow the mixture to come to room temperature, stirring it occasionally as it warms up to keep it emulsified. If the mixture is still solid once it has reached room temperature, gently reheat it in a mixing bowl placed over a pan of simmering water (do not allow the bowl to touch the water) until the desired consistency is achieved, stirring often as the mixture melts to ensure emulsification. You can also reheat the mixture in 20-second intervals in the microwave, whisking vigorously by hand after each interval, until the proper consistency is achieved. Remember that like chocolate, both ganache and caramel hold residual heat, so it is better to stop heating these mixtures before they have fully melted, as the residual heat will continue to soften the mixture.

- **SAVING A BROKEN GANACHE:** If the ganache has separated, remove the bowl from the heat, and using an immersion blender or food processor, blend the ganache with a very small amount of cold heavy cream. The emulsified cold cream should bring the broken ganache back together.

- **STRAINING PRESERVES:** Often when fruit preserves are used in a cake's filling or decor, it is necessary to strain the solid bits of fruit out first. This makes for a more homogenous mixture with a smoother texture. First you should warm the preserves gently, and then pour them through a strainer, pressing lightly on the solids to extract all liquid.

- **USING A CAKE BOARD FOR ASSEMBLY:** At the bakery, we always use a cardboard cake round when assembling any layer cake because many of the syrups we use to soak the cake layers are high in acid (passion fruit, blood orange, lemon, etc.), which can react with an aluminum cake pan bottom if it sits for an extended period of time. It is also easier for a home baker to build a cake directly onto the cardboard cake round from which it will eventually be served, instead of having to transfer an assembled cake later and risk dropping it. This is a very simple step: Simply place the correct size cardboard cake round into the bottom of the corresponding size cake pan in place of the pan's removable bottom or click the sides into place around it to lock it in place if using a springform pan. Assemble the cake on top of the cake round as if it were the metal bottom of the pan.

- **ASSEMBLING A CAKE:** If you are not familiar with the concept of building a cake inside a cake ring, this may seem a bit strange or daunting. It is the way professional pastry chefs build desserts and it actually results in not only an easier cake to frost and decorate, but also a visually more appealing cake when sliced. By containing the layers within the cake mold as you assemble the cake, the filling cannot spread out. Additionally, the top rim of the cake pan acts as a leveler and prevents the baker from assembling a lopsided cake. Freezing the cakes overnight before unmolding them allows the filling to firm up and yields a smoother surface on which to spread the frosting or cover with glaze, giving even the most inexperienced decorator a better chance of success.

- **SOAKING WITH SYRUP:** Cake layers are most absorbent immediately after baking and cooling, and will always, regardless of when they were baked, absorb more liquid on a side that is freshly cut. For this reason, always place cake layers cut side up during assembly before soaking with syrup. I have given exact amounts of syrup for each cake, and unless otherwise noted, you should evenly divide the amount of syrup among the layers being soaked. To some extent, the amount of syrup used really depends on how moist, or wet, you prefer your cake.

PIPING WITH STAR TIPS ON THE TOP OF A TORTAMISU (TOP) AND A BANANA CREAM TORTE (BOTTOM)

PIPING VERTICAL DESIGN AROUND THE SIDES OF A CAKE USING A PASTRY BAG WITH A STAR TIP

- **PIPING FILLINGS OR DECORATIVE FROSTINGS:** Using a pastry bag to pipe fillings onto cake layers instead of spreading them with a spatula ensures a more even layer and adds a decorative touch, seen only once the cake is sliced. And you can easily use a heavy-duty freezer bag instead of a fancy pastry bag: Cut a small hole (¼ to ½ inch wide) in one corner. Place a decorating tip into this hole, or use without a tip if you prefer. Simply fill the freezer bag the same way as a pastry bag and seal the bag closed. To pipe, close your dominant hand around the fattest part of the filled bag, as if you were holding an apple. Holding the decorating tip approximately 1 inch above where you are piping, use your other hand to gently guide the tip of the filled bag and help to hold the tip steady, squeezing the bag gently and evenly to push the filling or frosting through the tip. If piping spirals, start at the center of the circle and pipe steadily, moving in a counter-clockwise direction. If piping rosettes, make short, quick circles, flicking the wrist of the hand you use to grasp the pastry bag. When finished, just throw the bag away (remembering to remove the pastry tip first if one is used!).

- **TOASTING CAKE TRIMMINGS TO MAKE CAKE CRUMBS:** Preheat the oven to 350°F. Arrange the cake trimmings in a single layer on a baking sheet in the center of the oven and bake until lightly browned and dry. This should take between 10 and 20 minutes, depending on the amount of pieces being toasted. Once fully cooled, pulse in a food processor to make fine crumbs. Store the crumbs in an airtight container until ready to use or up to 5 days.

- **UNMOLDING A FROZEN ASSEMBLED CAKE:** This technique applies to all the cakes in this book, regardless of degree of assembly or type of pan it is being removed from. There are three ways to unmold a frozen cake:

1. Use a hair dryer set on high to gently heat the outside of the cake pan. Rotate the cake pan or circle it with the hair dryer so that the hair dryer heats up the entire outside. Be careful not to overheat—you want to create a very small amount of heat, just enough to start to melt the outside of the cake to soften it and allow it to release from the side of the pan.

2. If you have a gas stovetop, you can rotate the cake pan sideways over the open flame of a gas range.

3. Wrap a warm moist towel around the outside of the cake pan until the cake has softened enough to pop out of the pan.

- **EDGING A CAKE:** Cake crumbs, chocolate shavings, coconut flakes, and nuts are just some of the garnishes you can use to add a finished look and interesting textural contrast to a decorated cake. The technique for edging a cake is the same regardless of the item used to accomplish this: Place the crumbs (or shavings or flakes) on a wide plate or in a wide shallow bowl. Place the cake on a revolving cake stand or hold the decorated cake in one hand and at a slight angle over the plate of crumbs. Scoop up a handful of crumbs with your free hand and gently press them into the side of the cake, allowing the excess to drop back into the plate of crumbs. Rotate the cake as you continue to press crumbs into the side until the sides of the cake have been fully covered.

USING A HAIR DRYER TO UNMOLD A FROZEN CAKE

EDGING A CAKE WITH SHORTBREAD CRUMBS (TOP) AND ALMONDS (BOTTOM)

- **TIMING THE PROCESS:** At the end of each recipe I specify how long to leave a particular cake in the refrigerator (or at room temperature) before serving. The main point is to account for enough time between unmolding/frosting and serving to allow the interior of the frozen cake to fully thaw. Because these cakes are quite large and complex, this will be a minimum of 6 to 8 hours in the refrigerator. Unless otherwise specified in a particular recipe, most of these cakes can sit out at room temperature for 1 to 2 hours before being served without the risk of weeping or softening too much to cut.

- **MAKING CHOCOLATE SHAVINGS:** Heat a large (12-by-18-inch) rimmed baking sheet in the oven until it is just warm to the touch. Using an offset spatula, evenly coat the bottom of the pan with melted chocolate. Place the pan in the refrigerator to allow the chocolate to firm up. When firm, remove the pan from the refrigerator and as the chocolate begins to soften slightly, using a clean paint scraper, make shavings.

- **WORKING WITH GOLD LEAF:** I use 23kt edible gold leaf to decorate and enhance many of my desserts. It can be applied with your fingertips or a brush to the top of a whole cake or applied on flowers adorning the cake or plated presentation.

- **SLICING AND SERVING:** I recommend using a large, sharp hot knife to slice these cakes. You can heat the knife by immersing the blade in very hot water for a few seconds and wiping it dry before cutting each slice. You may also want to serve these cake slices on slightly larger plates, as most slices may be approximately 5 inches high. Each 10-inch cake will easily and generously serve 14 to 16 people, but you can adjust your serving sizes to more or less as you like. Sauces for many of these cakes can be found on pages 168 to 170.

GLAZING THE TOP OF THE CAKE WITH A
NARROW FLEXIBLE LEVELER

MAKING AND PLACING ROSE-PETAL
RIBBON STRAPS

SPRINKLING COCOA POWDER ON TOP OF
A CAKE USING A STRAINER

PLACING FRESH ROSE PETALS ONTO
A FINISHED CAKE

DECORATING THE CAKE

Each cake in this book calls for its own decoration. However, you should also feel free to mix and match techniques and come up with your own style and designs. At Extraordinary Desserts, all our cakes are presented on beautiful cake stands, lavishly garnished with fresh flowers, decorated with bits of edible gold leaf, and served with a sauce or coulis.

I choose the fresh flowers used as decor on the cakes based on the season. Of course, it's essential to choose a flower that will hold up for hours after cut. From there, I decide what color flower is most appropriate for the flavors and look of the cake. I also consider whether it is a birthday, wedding, or a simple dinner party, which gives me a sense of how elaborate the flowers will be. Sometimes a simple bloom from the garden propped on top of a finished cake is just the right flourish. I will leave it to you to add your own creative touches, and have offered up a basic flower guideline below to get you started. Remember to use pesticide-free flowers and advise your guests that the flowers are a visual decoration only and are not meant to be eaten.

FLOWERS FOR DECORATING CAKES

ARTICHOKE
Available: Year round
Used on: Holiday Yule Log (page 139)

BRAZILIAN BERRIES
Available: Spring, Summer, Winter
Used on: Holiday Yule Log (page 139)

CARNATION
Available: Year round
Used on: New York, New York (page 108)

DAHLIA
Available: Spring, Summer, Fall
Used on: Devika (page 39)

GARDENIA
Available: Year round
Used on: Chocolate Nirvana (page 71)

HYDRANGEA
Available: Year round
Used on: Decadent Yogi (page 47), Marco Polo (page 50), Tortamisù (page 120)

HYPERICUM
Available: Year round
Used on: Holiday Yule Log (page 139)

OBAKE
Available: Year round
Used on: Chocolate Nirvana (page 71)

ORCHID: CYMBIDIUM
Available: Year round
Used on: Bora Bora (page 89)

ORCHID: PHALAENOPSIS
Available: Year round
Used on: Bonaparte (page 159)

ORCHID: PURPLE MOKARA
Available: Year round
Used on: Diamond Head (page 67)

PEONY
Available: Winter, Spring
Used on: Strawberry Poppy Seed Cake (page 98)

RANUNCULUS
Available: Winter, Spring
Used on: Versailles (page 135)

ROSE
Available: Year round
Used on: Toutes Fraises (page 27), Dame Chocolat (page 31), Strawberry Shortcakes (page 80), Banana Cream Cake (page 113), Amor Chocolat (page 151)

SAGE
Available: Year round
Used on: White Chocolate Raspberry Linzer Torte (page 145)

SEEDED EUCALYPTUS
Available: Year round
Used on: Versailles (page 135)

SNOWBERRIES
Available: Winter
Used on: White Chocolate Raspberry Linzer Torte (page 145)

SPRAY ROSE
Available: Year round
Used on: Lemon Praline Torte (page 21), Devika (page 39)

STEPHANOTIS
Available: Year round
Used on: Lemon Ricotta (page 75)

SUNFLOWER
Available: Year round
Used on: New York, New York (page 108)

TULIPS
Available: Year round
Used on: Ivoire Royale (page 34), Marco Polo (page 50)

WAX FLOWER
Available: Fall, Winter, Spring
Used on: Lemon Praline Torte (page 21)

Extraordinary
SPRING

Lemon Praline Torte

The cake version of a lemon-lover's candy bar, this creamy and candy-coated torte features an unexpected crunch in the center. It can be served year round but is especially popular during Passover because matzo flour can substitute for all-purpose flour.

The cake base itself is a Génoise, which is a traditional French type of sponge cake made with many eggs and no chemical leavening. It soaks up syrup flavorings beautifully. I make use of two different kinds of meringue here, for contrasting textures. French meringue consists of egg whites whipped with sugar, whereas Italian meringue consists of egg whites whipped with a hot syrup that results in a sticky fluff.

For a colorful and complementary garnish, fresh berries or many of the fruit sauces included in this book are ideal (pages 168–170). The decoration gives the appearance of a wrapped gift box, and will require the use of floral glue and roses. For a simpler presentation, omit the floral straps and place several large roses atop the cake.

GÉNOISE

MAKES ONE 8-INCH SQUARE CAKE

SERVES 15

¼ cup unsalted butter, melted and warm, plus 2 teaspoons, melted but not hot, for greasing

10 large eggs

1 cup granulated sugar

1½ cups all-purpose flour, sifted

1. Preheat the oven to 300°F. Grease the bottom and sides of an 8-inch square cake pan with 2 teaspoons of the melted butter and line the bottom with a square of parchment paper.

2. Combine the eggs and sugar in a heatproof, nonreactive mixing bowl set over a saucepan of simmering water (do not allow the bowl to touch the water). Using a hand whisk, whip continuously until the mixture is warm to the touch and frothy, about 4 minutes.

3. Remove the bowl from over the water and transfer to a stand mixer fitted with the whisk attachment. Whip the mixture on high speed until light in color and tripled in volume, 7 to 10 minutes. Remove the bowl from the mixer. Using a rubber spatula, gently fold the sifted flour into the cooled batter in several additions.

4. Pour ¼ cup melted warm butter into a mixing bowl. Fold approximately one-third of the batter into the warm butter until incorporated. Gently fold this mixture back into the remaining batter, being careful not to deflate the mixture. Fold just until incorporated.

5. Pour the batter into the prepared cake pan and place on a rack in the center of the oven. Bake until the cake begins to pull away slightly from the sides of the pan and springs back slightly when pressed, about 55 minutes.

6. Remove the cake from the oven and allow to cool completely. Once cooled, remove the cake from the pan (see page 12) and peel the parchment paper from the bottom of the cake. Wrap the cake tightly in plastic wrap until ready to use. The Génoise can be made 1 day in advance and stored at room temperature.

LEMON SIMPLE SYRUP

¼ cup granulated sugar

½ cup freshly squeezed
lemon juice, strained

1. Combine the sugar and ⅛ cup water in a small, heavy saucepan over medium-high heat and bring to a boil, stirring occasionally. Remove from the heat, pour into a clean bowl, and allow to cool.

2. Once fully cooled, stir in the lemon juice until combined. The Lemon Simple Syrup will keep for up to 1 day in an airtight container in the refrigerator.

LEMON CURD

¾ cup freshly squeezed
lemon juice, strained

1½ cups granulated sugar

Grated zest of 2 lemons

6 large eggs

¾ cup unsalted butter,
room temperature,
cut into ¼-inch cubes

1. Combine the first 4 ingredients in a heatproof, nonreactive mixing bowl set over a pan of simmering water (do not allow the bowl to touch the water). Cook, whisking continuously, until the mixture is frothy and begins to thicken to a custard, about 4 minutes. If using a candy thermometer, cook to 190°F.

2. Remove the bowl from over the water and whisk in the butter until fully combined. The curd should be smooth and homogenous. Strain through a fine-mesh sieve into a clean, nonreactive mixing bowl. Measure out ½ cup of the Lemon Curd for the Lemon Buttercream recipe. The remainder will be used for assembling the cake. Cover all with plastic wrap pressed directly onto the surface of the curd and cool in the refrigerator until ready to use. The Lemon Curd can be made up to 3 days in advance.

ITALIAN MERINGUE

2 large egg whites

Scant ⅔ cup granulated sugar

1. In the bowl of a stand mixer fitted with the whisk attachment, whip the egg whites on medium speed for 2 minutes. When the egg whites are frothy, slowly add 3 tablespoons of the sugar and increase the mixer speed to medium-high. Whip until the egg whites are stiff with a creamy texture, about 3 minutes. If you reach a stiff meringue before the sugar has fully cooked (see step 2, below), reduce the mixer speed to low until the hot sugar syrup is ready.

2. While the whites are whipping, combine the remaining sugar and 3 tablespoons water in a small, heavy saucepan and bring to a boil. Insert a candy thermometer and cook to 230° to 240°F, the soft-ball stage.

3. With the mixer on medium-high speed, carefully pour the hot syrup into the whipping meringue in a continuous stream, being careful to avoid pouring the syrup directly onto the moving whisk. Increase the mixer speed to high and whisk until the meringue has cooled down, about 4 minutes. Once cooled, the meringue should have a thick and gooey consistency.

4. Transfer the Italian Meringue to a clean container and cover with plastic wrap. Store in the refrigerator if using the same day. It may also be stored in an airtight container in the freezer for up to 5 days if making in advance. The Italian Meringue can be used frozen.

½ cup whole milk

½ teaspoon vanilla extract

Scant ¾ cup granulated sugar

8 large egg yolks

2⅓ cups unsalted butter,
room temperature,
cut into ¼-inch cubes

1 recipe Italian Meringue

½ cup Lemon Curd

Grated zest of 2 lemons

¼ cup freshly squeezed
lemon juice, strained

1. In a medium, heavy saucepan over medium-high heat, bring the milk, vanilla, and 6 tablespoons of the sugar to a boil.

2. Meanwhile, whisk together the remaining sugar and the egg yolks in a heatproof, nonreactive mixing bowl until well combined and smooth. While whisking continuously, slowly pour the warm milk mixture into the egg mixture and whisk until well incorporated.

3. Return the milk-egg mixture to the saucepan, insert a candy thermometer, and cook over medium heat, stirring gently with a rubber spatula, until the mixture begins to thicken and has reached 150°F. This should take 3 to 4 minutes.

4. Strain the mixture through a fine-mesh sieve into the clean bowl of a stand mixer fitted with the whisk attachment. Whip on medium-high speed until cooled, thickened, and pale yellow in color, about 6 minutes.

5. Reduce the mixer speed to low and add the butter, ½ cup at a time, until fully incorporated. Add the Italian Meringue, increasing the mixer speed as necessary to fully incorporate. Once fully combined, remove the bowl from the mixer. Using a rubber spatula, fold in the Lemon Curd, followed by the lemon zest and juice. Whisk the Lemon Buttercream by hand until smooth.

6. Reserve 1½ cups of the Lemon Buttercream in a separate container to be used for the final Decor. Cover all with plastic wrap and if you are not using immediately, refrigerate until ready to use but for no longer than 24 hours, because the lemon flavor can change. If refrigerated, allow the Lemon Buttercream to come to room temperature before using or gently reheat the buttercream in the microwave in eight 10- to 20-second intervals, whisking vigorously by hand after each interval, to obtain the buttercream's original texture.

1 teaspoon unsalted butter,
melted but not hot,
for greasing paper

3 large egg whites

⅓ cup granulated sugar

¾ cup powdered sugar, sifted

1. Preheat the oven to 250°F. Using a pencil, trace a 7-inch square onto a sheet of parchment paper. Flip the paper over, pencil side down, onto a baking sheet. Using a pastry brush, coat the traced square with the melted butter.

2. In the bowl of a stand mixer fitted with the whisk attachment, whip the egg whites on medium speed for 2 minutes. When the egg whites are frothy, begin to slowly add in the granulated sugar and increase the mixer speed to medium-high. Whip until the egg whites are stiff with a creamy texture, about 3 minutes. Remove the bowl from the mixer.

3. Using a rubber spatula, fold in the sifted powdered sugar in two additions, incorporating well each time. The French Meringue should be very white and thick. Fit a pastry bag with a ½-inch plain round decorating tip and fill with French Meringue. Pipe the meringue over the traced square on the prepared parchment to cover completely.

4. Place the baking sheet on a rack in the center of the oven and bake for approximately 55 minutes. The meringue will turn a slightly beige color and will become very hard and crusty outside, yet still be soft and chewy inside.

5. Remove the meringue from the oven and allow to cool completely. The baked French Meringue may be stored overnight if in a very dry area, such as inside a cool oven.

ASSEMBLY

Génoise, baked and cooled

1 recipe Lemon Simple
Syrup

2½ to 3 cups Lemon
Buttercream

1½ cups Lemon Curd

French Meringue,
baked and cooled

1. Place the unwrapped Génoise on a flat work surface. Using a long serrated knife, slice off the top ¼ inch to even out the top of the cake as necessary. Slice the cake horizontally into 2 even ¼- to ½-inch-thick layers.

2. Using an 8-inch square cake board as the bottom of an 8-inch square cake pan with removable bottom (see page 13), place one cake layer on the cake board, cut side up. Using a pastry brush, moisten the top of the cake layer with one-half of the Lemon Simple Syrup.

3. Using an offset spatula, spread 1 cup of the Lemon Buttercream evenly onto the syrup-soaked cake layer and top with ¾ cup of the Lemon Curd. Cover with the baked French Meringue layer, piped side down, so that it is flat on top. Repeat with 1 cup of the Lemon Buttercream and the remaining Lemon Curd.

4. Top with a second cake layer and moisten with the remaining Lemon Simple Syrup. Using a long metal spatula, cover with the remaining Lemon Buttercream, spreading it very evenly over the cake. It is important to spread this layer as smoothly as possible, as this will be the top of the cake. Tightly wrap the cake in the pan in plastic wrap and place in the freezer overnight.

1 tablespoon grapeseed
or vegetable oil

1¼ cups granulated sugar

¼ cup hazelnuts,
toasted and cooled

⅓ cup almonds,
toasted and cooled

1. Generously coat a baking sheet with the oil or line the baking sheet with a Silpat and set aside.

2. Place the sugar in a small, heavy saucepan over medium-high heat. As the sugar begins to melt, use a wooden spoon or rubber spatula to stir it every 30 seconds. After 3 to 5 minutes, the sugar should begin to caramelize and turn a light amber color. Once the sugar becomes liquid, insert a candy thermometer and cook until the syrup reaches 320° to 330°F, at which point it should have turned deep amber in color. This should take about 3 minutes.

3. Remove the pan from the heat and set the candy thermometer aside. Using a heatproof rubber spatula, quickly stir in the toasted nuts, mixing well to fully and evenly coat in caramel. Carefully spread the hot mixture onto the prepared baking sheet to cool. Do not grind up the cooled praline until you are ready for the final Decor. The Hazelnut Almond Praline should be made the day it is to be used.

1 recipe Hazelnut
Almond Praline

Reserved 1½ cups
Lemon Buttercream

4 (7-inch-long) strips of
1½-inch-wide satin ribbon

Floral glue

18 to 24 small, medium, and large
roses

8 pearlhead pins

Blackberry, Raspberry,
Strawberry, Kiwi, or
Mango Sauce (pages 168–170)
(optional)

1. Remove the assembled cake from the freezer, remove the plastic wrap, and unmold the cake from the pan (see page 14). Transfer the cake to a clean 8-inch square cake board (optional).

2. Break apart the cooled praline. In 2 separate batches, grind the praline pieces to a fine powder in a food processor fitted with the blade attachment.

3. Using an offset spatula, frost the sides and top of the cake with the reserved Lemon Buttercream. Press the ground Hazelnut Almond Praline evenly onto the sides and over the top of the cake to completely cover the buttercream. Repeat as necessary for a well-covered, crunchy look.

4. Working with one strip of ribbon at a time, spray one side of the ribbon with the floral glue and quickly stick 15 to 20 rose petals of varying sizes onto each piece (see page 17). Lay one rose-petal ribbon from the center down each side of the cake, securing each piece with a pin at the bottom and top edges, hiding pins under petals.

5. Place the cake centered on a plate. In the middle of the cake, arrange the roses that remain whole after you have made the petal strips. Poke the roses directly into the cake top, at the point where the ribbons intersect, trimming the stems if necessary.

6. Store the decorated cake in the refrigerator for up to 6 hours, until ready to display or serve. Allow the cake to come to room temperature for 1 to 2 hours before serving. Serve slices with sauce, if desired.

Toute Fraises

I first made these cupcakes for my daughter, Sahara, on her fifth birthday, and the recipe has become one of my most cherished. Pink is Sahara's favorite color and she loves everything strawberry. The delight on her face when she saw these matched the enthusiasm with which she ate them!

Here, a traditional cupcake is combined with the European practice of filling desserts with fresh fruit or preserves to create a moist, vanilla-flavored cupcake enriched with chopped strawberries and a preserve filling.

These are best when baked, frosted, and served the same day, particularly when using fresh berries. The dehydrated strawberries can be replaced with fresh strawberries, and dehydrated or fresh raspberries produce equally delicious results. Filling the centers with preserves is optional, but truly adds a sweet surprise.

STRAWBERRY CUPCAKES

MAKES 14 CUPCAKES

1¾ cups all-purpose flour

1 teaspoon baking powder

½ teaspoon baking soda

Pinch of salt

⅓ cup plus 2 tablespoons unsalted butter, room temperature, cut into ¼-inch cubes

1 teaspoon honey

½ cup granulated sugar

¼ cup (loosely packed) light brown sugar

2 large eggs

1 teaspoon vanilla extract

1 cup sour cream, room temperature

¾ cup dehydrated strawberries, or 1 cup fresh strawberries, hulled and diced

¼ cup seedless or strained strawberry preserves

½ teaspoon freshly squeezed lemon juice

1. Preheat the oven to 250°F. Line a 14-cup muffin pan with paper liners.

2. Sift together the flour, baking powder, baking soda, and salt.

3. In the bowl of a stand mixer fitted with the paddle attachment, cream the butter, honey, and both sugars for 5 minutes on medium-high speed. Add the eggs and vanilla and continue mixing for another 3 to 5 minutes. Scrape down the sides of the bowl and beat for another 3 minutes. The mixture will be very light, fluffy, and smooth.

4. Reduce the mixer speed to low. Incorporate the sour cream and sifted dry ingredients in 4 additions, alternating between each and starting with the sour cream. Mix just until combined. Remove the bowl from the mixer. Using a rubber spatula, fold in the strawberries, being careful not to overmix.

5. Using a ⅓-cup dry measure, scoop the batter into the paper liners.

6. Bake the cupcakes on a rack in the center of the oven until slightly brown and firm to the touch, 25 to 30 minutes. The blade of a knife should come out clean when inserted into the center of the cakes. Remove the cupcakes from the oven and let cool for 30 minutes.

7. Once cooled, use your index finger to poke a hole in the center of each cupcake, creating a cavity.

8. In a small bowl, stir together the strawberry preserves and lemon juice to combine. Fill a resealable plastic bag with preserves, seal the bag, and cut a small hole in one corner to mimic a pastry bag. Use this to fill each cavity with approximately 1 teaspoon of the preserve mixture.

9. If serving the same day, set the filled cupcakes aside until ready to frost, or store them in the refrigerator in an airtight container or tightly wrapped in plastic wrap for up to 1 day before frosting.

¾ cup unsalted butter, room temperature, cut into 6 pieces

3 cups powdered sugar, sifted

2 teaspoons vanilla extract

1¼ cups (from two 8-ounce packages) cream cheese, room temperature

2 tablespoons strained strawberry preserves

½ teaspoon freshly squeezed lemon juice

1. In the bowl of a stand mixer fitted with the paddle attachment, beat together the butter and powdered sugar on medium-high speed until creamy, about 3 minutes. Reduce the mixer speed to low, scrape down the sides of the bowl, and add the vanilla, then the cream cheese. Mix just until well blended, about 2 minutes. Remove the bowl from the mixer.

2. Using a rubber spatula, stir the frosting by hand to ensure there are no lumps. Chill the frosting in the refrigerator until firm, about 30 minutes.

3. In a small bowl, stir together the strawberry preserves and lemon juice to blend.

4. Remove the frosting from the refrigerator, and using a rubber spatula, lightly fold in the preserves to create a marbled appearance. The Strawberry Cream Cheese Frosting should be used as soon as it is made.

ASSEMBLY

Strawberry Cupcakes, baked and cooled

⅓ cup powdered sugar

1 recipe Strawberry Cream Cheese Frosting

1. Place the cupcakes on a flat work surface. Using a small sieve, sprinkle cupcakes with powdered sugar.

2. Fit a pastry bag with a ½-inch, 9-point closed star tip and fill with the Strawberry Cream Cheese Frosting. Pipe a 1½- to 2-inch-tall rosette on the top of each cupcake.

3. Place the decorated cupcakes in the refrigerator for 2 to 3 hours or overnight to allow the frosting to set.

DECOR

Fresh strawberry slices or fresh or candied rose petals (optional)

1. Remove the Strawberry Cupcakes from the refrigerator 1 hour before serving.

2. When ready to serve, top each rosette with a strawberry slice, fresh rose petal, or a candied rose petal, if desired.

Dame Chocolat

This grande dame of chocolate cakes is so rich between the layers that it reminds me of the opulent sweets displayed in European pastry shops. From the remarkably light flourless cake to the dark, intense mirroir glaze, it explodes with pure chocolate flavor. The use of high-cocoa-percentage chocolates in the mousse produces a temptingly bitter effect rarely found in American-style desserts. Because the génoise cake does not include flour, Dame Chocolat is gluten-free as well as sumptuous. To best appreciate its lovely creamy texture, prepare the Bittersweet Chocolate Mousse the day the cake will be assembled.

FLOURLESS CHOCOLATE GÉNOISE

MAKES ONE 8-INCH CAKE

SERVES 12

2 teaspoons unsalted butter, melted but not hot

4 large egg whites

Scant ⅔ cup granulated sugar

6 large egg yolks

½ cup cocoa powder, sifted

1. Preheat the oven to 325°F. Grease the bottom and sides of an 8-by-3-inch round cake pan with a removable bottom with the melted butter and line the bottom with an 8-inch-diameter parchment paper round.

2. In the bowl of a stand mixer fitted with the whisk attachment, whip the egg whites on medium speed for 2 minutes. When the egg whites are frothy, gradually add the sugar and increase the mixer speed to medium-high. Whip until the egg whites have doubled in volume, about 3 minutes.

3. Add the egg yolks one at a time, whisking just long enough between each addition to incorporate. Remove the bowl from the mixer, and using a rubber spatula, gently fold in the cocoa powder.

4. Pour the batter into the prepared cake pan and place on a rack in the center of the oven. Bake until the cake springs back slightly when pressed and the blade of an inserted knife or cake tester comes out cleanly, 30 to 35 minutes.

5. Remove the cake from the oven and allow to cool completely. Once cooled, remove the cake from the pan (see page 12) and peel the parchment paper from the bottom of the cake. Wrap the cake tightly in plastic wrap until ready to use. The Flourless Chocolate Génoise can be stored for up to 1 day at room temperature.

COCOA SIMPLE SYRUP

¼ cup granulated sugar

2 tablespoons cocoa powder, sifted

1. Combine the sugar with ¼ cup water in a small, heavy saucepan over medium-high heat and bring to a boil, stirring occasionally. Remove from the heat and stir in the cocoa powder until fully combined.

2. Strain the syrup through a fine-mesh sieve into a clean bowl and allow to cool. The Cocoa Simple Syrup will keep for up to 3 days in an airtight container in the refrigerator.

SEMISWEET CHOCOLATE GANACHE

12 ounces (2 cups)
semisweet chocolate chips

1 cup heavy cream

2 teaspoons Myer's dark rum

1. Place the chocolate chips in a medium, heatproof mixing bowl.

2. Bring the cream to a boil in a small, heavy saucepan over medium-high heat. Pour the hot cream over the chocolate and let sit for 5 minutes. Using a rubber spatula, stir slowly and gently in a circular motion until the mixture is fully combined and homogenous.

3. Transfer the chocolate mixture to a food processor; add the rum and process to blend (or, using an immersion blender, add the rum to the bowl with the chocolate and cream and blend to emulsify). The ganache should be thick and shiny.

4. Pour the ganache into a clean mixing bowl and allow to cool and firm to the consistency of pudding. The Semisweet Chocolate Ganache can be made up to 5 days in advance and kept in an airtight container in the refrigerator, but may need to be gently reheated before using (see page 12).

BITTERSWEET CHOCOLATE MOUSSE

2⅓ cups heavy cream

6 ounces (1 cup) 70% bittersweet chocolate, coarsely chopped

3 ounces (½ cup) 64% bittersweet chocolate, coarsely chopped

½ cup granulated sugar

2 large eggs

6 large egg yolks

1. In the bowl of a stand mixer fitted with the whisk attachment, whip the cream until soft peaks form, about 2 minutes. Hold in the refrigerator until ready to use.

2. Combine both chocolates in a heatproof mixing bowl set over a pan of simmering water (do not allow the bowl to touch the water). Stir occasionally until melted.

3. Combine the sugar with 3 tablespoons water in a small, heavy saucepan and bring to a boil over medium-high heat. Insert a candy thermometer and cook to 230° to 240°F, the soft-ball stage.

4. While the sugar is cooking, combine the eggs and the yolks in the bowl of a stand mixer fitted with the whisk attachment and whip at medium-high speed until thick and light, 2 to 3 minutes.

5. Carefully pour the hot sugar syrup into the whipping eggs in a continuous stream, being careful to avoid pouring the syrup directly onto the moving whisk. Increase the mixer speed to high and whip until the mixture has cooled down and tripled in volume, 7 to 10 minutes. Remove the bowl from the mixer.

6. Using a whisk, vigorously mix half of the melted chocolate into the egg mixture. Using a rubber spatula, fold half of the whipped cream into the chocolate-egg mixture. Repeat with the remaining chocolate and then the remaining whipped cream. To retain its creamy texture, it is best to make this mousse the same day as assembling the cake. If you must make it a few hours in advance, cover it with plastic wrap and keep it refrigerated.

Flourless Chocolate Génoise, baked and cooled

1 recipe Cocoa Simple Syrup

1 recipe Semisweet Chocolate Ganache

1 recipe Bittersweet Chocolate Mousse

1. Place the unwrapped cake on a flat work surface. Using a long serrated knife, trim approximately ½ inch off the circumference of the cake to make it a 7-inch-diameter round. Next, slice the cake horizontally into 2 equal layers. You should have 2 cake layers that are smaller in diameter than the cake pan in which the cake will be assembled. When assembling the dessert, the mousse layer will actually go in between the cake and the pan and form the outside coating of the finished cake.

2. Using an 8-inch cake board as the bottom of an 8-by-3-inch cake pan with removable bottom (see page 13), place 1 cake layer on the cake board, cut side up. Using a pastry brush, moisten the cake layer with one-half of the Cocoa Simple Syrup.

3. Using an offset spatula, spread approximately ½ cup of the cooled Semisweet Chocolate Ganache evenly over the top of the syrup-soaked cake layer, being careful to not push any over the side. Top with 3 cups of Bittersweet Chocolate Mousse. If necessary, use a small spatula to push the mousse firmly down in between the side of the cake and the side of the pan.

4. Top with the second layer of cake and repeat with the remaining Cocoa Simple Syrup, ½ cup of the ganache, and the remaining mousse. Tightly wrap the cake in the pan in plastic wrap and place in the freezer overnight. The cake can be stored in the freezer for up to 3 days at this point. Cover and refrigerate the remaining Semisweet Chocolate Ganache until ready to finish the cake.

5. Remove the assembled cake from the freezer and remove the plastic wrap.

6. Gently reheat the remaining ganache until softened. Using a long metal spatula, evenly spread the ganache over the top of the mousse, making it level with the rim of the cake pan (see page 17). Tightly wrap the pan in plastic and place in the freezer overnight.

DECOR

Dark Chocolate Mirroir (page 155)

Fresh flowers or flower petals, as desired

Chocolate Sauce (page 169) (optional)

1. Remove the cake from the freezer and remove the plastic wrap. Pour approximately ½ cup of the Dark Chocolate Mirroir onto the top of the still-frozen cake and use a long metal spatula to smooth it out evenly (see page 17). Return the cake to the freezer for 10 minutes to set. When set, repeat with the remaining mirroir so that the top of the cake is very evenly finished. Return the cake to the freezer for another 10 minutes to set.

2. Remove the cake from the freezer and carefully unmold the cake from the pan (see page 14). Place the unmolded cake directly onto a cake plate and decorate with fresh flowers as desired. Allow the cake to thaw in the refrigerator for 6 hours.

3. Remove the decorated cake from the refrigerator up to 1 hour before serving to allow the cake to soften. Serve slices with sauce, if desired.

Ivoire Royale

This simple yet elegant cake is perfect for special occasions. Because of its stunning appearance and extraordinary taste, it is a favorite for weddings, anniversaries, showers, and birthdays. The combination of white cake and white chocolate with red and blue berries is very festive, and the creaminess of the mousse-filled layers contrasts well with the sweet-tart fruit.

When making the cake batter and the mousse, the sour cream should be at room temperature so that it folds in easily. Also remember that once you have made the whipped cream, it must be used immediately.

While not difficult to master, the decor requires some confidence with a pastry bag. As an easier option, toast any extra cake cut off during assembly, grind the pieces into crumbs, and use them to edge the sides (see page 15). The top can be finished with simple rosettes and a sprinkling of fresh berries. You also can omit the white chocolate shavings.

SOUR CREAM POUND CAKE

MAKES ONE 10-INCH CAKE

SERVES 14 TO 16

2 teaspoons unsalted
butter, melted but not hot

6 large eggs

2 cups granulated sugar

1 cup grapeseed
or vegetable oil

1 cup sour cream,
room temperature

1 teaspoon freshly
squeezed lemon juice

½ teaspoon vanilla extract

3 cups all-purpose flour

3 teaspoons baking powder

1. Preheat the oven to 300°F. Grease the bottom and sides of a 10-by-3-inch round cake pan with removable bottom with the melted butter and line the bottom with a 10-inch-diameter parchment paper round.

2. In the bowl of a stand mixer fitted with the whisk attachment, whip together the eggs and sugar at medium-high speed until the mixture is very thick and lightens in color, about 7 minutes.

3. In a separate mixing bowl, whisk together the oil, sour cream, lemon juice, and vanilla. Add the sour cream mixture to the eggs and sugar and whip just until blended.

4. Sift together the flour and baking powder. Add the sifted ingredients to the batter, mixing just until incorporated, scraping down the sides of the mixing bowl as needed. Do not overmix. If necessary, finish folding in the sifted ingredients by hand.

5. Pour the batter into the prepared cake pan and place on a rack in the center of the oven. Bake the cake until golden brown, about 90 minutes. The top of the cake may crack while baking. The cake is done when a knife blade inserted into the center comes out clean and when the top of the cake springs back lightly when touched.

6. Remove the cake from the oven and allow to cool completely. Once cooled, remove the cake from the pan (see page 12) and peel the parchment paper from the bottom of the cake. Wrap the cake tightly in plastic wrap until ready to use. The Sour Cream Pound Cake can be stored for up to 1 day in the refrigerator or in the freezer for up to 1 week.

VANILLA SIMPLE SYRUP

½ cup granulated sugar

3 tablespoons vanilla extract

1. Combine the sugar with ½ cup water in a small, heavy saucepan over medium-high heat and bring to a boil, stirring occasionally. Remove from the heat, pour into a clean bowl, and allow to cool.

2. Once fully cooled, stir in the vanilla and 2 tablespoons water until combined. The Vanilla Simple Syrup will keep for up to 3 days in an airtight container in the refrigerator.

WHITE CHOCOLATE SOUR CREAM MOUSSE

1 cup sour cream, room temperature

6.5 ounces (1¼ cups) good-quality white chocolate, chopped

1¼ cups heavy cream

1. Place the sour cream in a mixing bowl and whisk quickly to loosen. If the sour cream is colder than room temperature, gently warm it in a microwave.

2. Place the chocolate in a medium, heatproof mixing bowl.

3. Bring the heavy cream to a boil in a small, heavy saucepan over medium-high heat. Pour the hot cream over the white chocolate and let sit for a couple of minutes before whisking until smooth and fully combined.

4. Using a hand whisk, mix the sour cream into the white chocolate ganache in 2 additions. Cover with plastic wrap pressed directly onto the surface of the White Chocolate Sour Cream Mousse and refrigerate overnight to set. The White Chocolate Sour Cream Mousse can be made up to 2 days in advance and stored in the refrigerator, tightly covered, until ready to use. This mousse recipe can be used cold, directly from the refrigerator.

ASSEMBLY

1 pint fresh strawberries

3 cups heavy cream

¼ cup granulated sugar

Sour Cream Pound Cake, baked and cooled

1 recipe Vanilla Simple Syrup

1 recipe White Chocolate Sour Cream Mousse

1 cup each fresh raspberries, blackberries, and blueberries

1. Hull approximately 8 medium-sized strawberries and slice each into 10 to 12 pieces.

2. In the bowl of a stand mixer fitted with the whisk attachment, whip together the cream and the sugar until stiff peaks form, 2 to 3 minutes. The whipped cream must be used immediately so it does not lose its volume and soften. Fit a pastry bag with a ½-inch plain round decorating tip and fill with half of the whipped cream.

3. Place the unwrapped pound cake on a flat work surface. Using a long serrated knife, slice off the top ¼ inch to even out the top of the cake as necessary. Set the cut piece aside to be used later as an option to edge the cake (see page 14). Slice the cake horizontally into 3 even layers.

4. Using a 10-inch round cake board as the bottom of a 10-by-3-inch round cake pan with removable bottom (see page 13), place 1 cake layer on the cake board, cut side up. Using a pastry brush, moisten the cake layer with one-third of the Vanilla Simple Syrup.

5. Using an offset spatula, cover the syrup-soaked cake layer with approximately one-quarter of the White Chocolate Sour Cream Mousse. Using the filled pastry bag, pipe a layer of whipped cream over the mousse in a spiral pattern, using the entire bag. Refill the bag with the remaining whipped cream to be used on the next layer. Sprinkle 1 cup raspberries and the sliced strawberries over the whipped cream.

6. Top with a second layer of cake and repeat with the syrup, mousse, and whipped cream. Sprinkle with 1 cup blueberries and 1 cup blackberries.

7. Top with the final layer of cake and moisten with the remaining Vanilla Simple Syrup. Using an offset spatula, spread the remaining White Chocolate Sour Cream Mousse evenly over the top of the cake. Tightly wrap the cake in the pan in plastic wrap and place in the freezer overnight.

DECOR

3 cups heavy cream

¼ cup granulated sugar

White chocolate shavings (see page 15) (optional)

¼ cup powdered sugar, sifted

Blackberry Sauce or Raspberry Sauce (pages 168–170) (optional)

1. In the bowl of a stand mixer fitted with the whisk attachment, whip together the cream and the sugar until stiff peaks form, 2 to 3 minutes. Fit a pastry bag with a ¼-inch, 7-point star decorating tip and fill with half of the whipped cream.

2. Remove the assembled cake from the freezer, remove the plastic wrap, and unmold the cake from the pan (see page 14). Using an offset spatula, spread a ½-inch-thick layer of the remaining whipped cream around the sides and top of the cake as evenly as possible.

3. Using the prepared pastry bag and working in a clockwise direction, pipe straight lines around the side of the cake from the bottom edge to the top edge. Return the decorated cake to the refrigerator for 8 to 10 hours or overnight to thaw and to allow all of the fruit to fully defrost.

4. One hour before serving, remove the cake from the refrigerator and place on a doily-covered 12-inch round cake board or directly onto a cake plate. Finish decorating the cake using piles of white chocolate shavings, if desired. Fill a small sieve with the powdered sugar and generously dust the top of the cake (see page 17). Serve slices with sauce, if desired.

Devika

On a trip to Udaipur, India, I was delighted to discover that guests were welcomed with rose petals strewn about the hotels and resorts. Surrounded by luxurious sights and smells, the experience inspired me to re-create this warmth and generosity of spirit in pastry. *Devika* means "little goddess" in Sanskrit. I often serve these small cakes, made with rose essence to capture the flavors and aroma of rose petals, after a wonderful outdoor meal celebrating our beautiful southern California sunsets.

I like to use almond flour because it creates an extremely moist, fine cake. However, I strongly recommend sifting this flour, as it tends to clump in the package. To make this recipe, you also will need rose syrup, and a square silicone savarin mold with eight cavities (see page 9). At Extraordinary Desserts, we first bake, cool, and unmold eight cakes, then bake the remaining four in the same pan for a total of 12. Due to the fruit content, these cannot be made more than one day in advance.

ROSE-FLAVORED TORTES

MAKES 12 INDIVIDUAL CAKES

SERVES 12

2 pints fresh raspberries

1 teaspoon rose syrup

2 tablespoons whole milk

1¾ cups almond flour

½ cup powdered sugar

½ cup all-purpose flour, sifted

1 cup unsalted butter,
room temperature, plus
2 teaspoons, melted but
not hot, for greasing mold

3 large egg yolks

1 large egg

2 large egg whites

3 tablespoons granulated sugar

1 pint fresh blackberries

2 pints fresh strawberries,
hulled and cut into ½-inch cubes

1. Preheat the oven to 300°F. Lightly grease a silicone square savarin mold (see page 9) with the 2 teaspoons melted butter.

2. Smash 6 to 8 raspberries and strain through a fine-mesh sieve into a small bowl to yield 1 teaspoon juice. Add the rose syrup and milk and set aside.

3. Sift together 1⅓ cups almond flour and the powdered sugar into a mixing bowl. Add the all-purpose flour and stir to blend.

4. In the bowl of a stand mixer fitted with the paddle attachment, beat the 1 cup butter until light and fluffy, about 3 minutes. Add the rose syrup mixture and then the egg yolks and whole egg, mixing well each time. Add the sifted dry ingredients, mixing just until combined. Transfer the batter to a clean mixing bowl large enough to mix in the meringue (see step 6).

5. In the bowl of a stand mixer fitted with the whisk attachment, whip the egg whites on medium speed for 2 minutes. When the egg whites are frothy, begin to slowly add the granulated sugar and increase the mixer speed to medium-high. Whip until the egg whites are stiff with a creamy texture, about 3 minutes. Remove the bowl from the mixer.

6. Using a rubber spatula, fold the meringue into the batter until evenly combined.

7. Place 3 tablespoons of the batter in each cavity of the savarin mold. Add 1 blackberry, 2 raspberries, and 2 small cubed pieces of strawberry to each batter-filled cavity and push the fruit gently into the batter.

8. Place the mold on a rack in the center of the oven and bake for about 55 minutes, until firm, or a knife tip inserted comes out clean.

9. Remove the tortes from the oven and allow to cool to room temperature. When fully cooled, remove the tortes from the savarin mold. They should easily pop out of each cavity. Using a sharp knife or scissors, trim the sides of each individual torte so that the edges are very even. During baking, the batter may rise and spill out of the mold slightly. This can create an uneven appearance and will make it difficult to decorate with the strawberries if not trimmed square after baking. Wrap each torte in plastic wrap until ready to use. The Rose-Flavored Tortes can be stored for up to 1 day in the refrigerator.

10. Reserve the remaining fresh berries to make the Berry Sauce (see Decor) that will be used when plating the individual tortes.

RASPBERRY GELÉE

⅓ cup raspberry jam

¼ cup granulated sugar

½ cup fresh raspberries

1 tablespoon glucose
or light corn syrup

Combine all the ingredients in a small, heavy saucepan over medium-high heat. Bring to a boil, insert a candy thermometer, and cook until the temperature reaches 220°F, about 4 minutes. Strain through a fine-mesh sieve into a clean bowl and allow to cool. One teaspoon of Raspberry Gelée will be dropped into the center of each square Rose-Flavored Torte and the remaining gelée will be used in the berry sauce. The Raspberry Gelée should be made the same day you plan to serve the cakes.

ROSE WHIPPED CREAM

2 cups heavy cream

1 tablespoon granulated sugar

1 tablespoon rose syrup

1. In the bowl of a stand mixer fitted with the whisk attachment, whip together the cream and sugar until stiff peaks form, about 2 minutes. Remove the bowl from the mixer.

2. Using a rubber spatula, fold in the rose syrup until fully combined and the whipped cream has taken on a pink tint. The Rose Whipped Cream should be made when ready to assemble the tortes.

12 Rose-Flavored Tortes,
baked and cooled

¼ cup Raspberry Gelée

1 recipe Rose Whipped Cream

24 equal-sized fresh strawberries

6 fresh raspberries

Fresh red spray roses (optional)

1. Place the unwrapped tortes on a flat work surface. Drop 1 teaspoon of the Raspberry Gelée into the center cavity of each Rose-Flavored Torte.

2. Fit a pastry bag with a ¼-inch, 7-point star decorating tip and fill with the Rose Whipped Cream. Pipe a large rosette onto the top of each torte, centering it over the Raspberry Gelée.

3. Using a paring knife, hull the strawberries and cut off the stem side so that each is flat on the bottom. Slice each strawberry into 4 thin, even pieces, discarding the sides if necessary. Pipe a small dot of whipped cream onto one side of each strawberry slice (the cream will help the strawberry adhere to the cake surface). Stick 2 slices onto each edge of each Rose-Flavored Torte, using a total of 8 strawberry slices per cake.

4. Using a paring knife, cut each raspberry in half. Top each rosette with half a raspberry and finish off with a rose petal or a strawberry slice.

5. Place the Rose-Flavored Tortes on a serving tray and refrigerate for 2 hours before serving, to allow the cakes to firm up and the flavors to fully develop. The tortes can be displayed at room temperature for up to 1 hour before serving.

DECOR

Remaining Raspberry Gelée

Reserved fresh berries from
Rose-Flavored Tortes recipe

1 cup frozen raspberries

1 tablespoon granulated sugar,
or to taste

Strawberry ice cream (optional)

1. Combine the first 4 ingredients in the bowl of a food processor fitted with the blade attachment and blend until smooth. Add more sugar as needed to taste. Strain the berry sauce though a fine-mesh sieve into a clean bowl. Cover with plastic wrap and refrigerate until ready to serve, or for up to 2 hours.

2. Serve each cake with fresh berry sauce and strawberry ice cream, if desired.

Viking

A favorite among chocolate fans, this is a study in pure decadence. When developing its many textures and layers of all things chocolate, I created the biggest, baddest chocolate dessert I could imagine, one as bold in flavor as the Vikings were in battle. Made of chocolate cake, chocolate chantilly (whipped cream), chocolate crème brûlée, chocolate almond praline, chocolate ganache, and chocolate shavings, the outrageous Viking more than fits the bill. Because this recipe is all about chocolate, use absolutely the best quality you can find.

CHOCOLATE SOUR CREAM CAKE

MAKES ONE 10-INCH CAKE | SERVES 14 TO 16 **(page 151)**

COCOA SIMPLE SYRUP

½ cup granulated sugar

¼ cup cocoa powder, sifted

1. Combine the sugar with ½ cup water in a small, heavy saucepan over medium-high heat and bring to a boil, stirring occasionally. Remove from the heat and stir in the cocoa powder until fully combined.

2. Strain the syrup through a fine-mesh sieve into a clean bowl and allow to cool. The Cocoa Simple Syrup will keep for up to 3 days in an airtight container in the refrigerator.

SEMISWEET CHOCOLATE GANACHE

24 ounces (4 cups) semisweet chocolate chips

2 cups heavy cream

1 tablespoon Myer's dark rum

1. Place the chocolate chips in a medium, heatproof mixing bowl.

2. Bring the cream to a boil in a small, heavy saucepan over medium-high heat. Pour the hot cream over the chocolate and let sit for 5 minutes. Using a rubber spatula, stir slowly and gently in a circular motion until the mixture is fully combined and homogenous.

3. Transfer the chocolate mixture to a food processor; add the rum and process to blend (or, using an immersion blender, add the rum to the bowl with the chocolate and cream and blend to emulsify). The ganache should be thick and shiny.

4. Measure out approximately 1¾ cups of the Semisweet Chocolate Ganache and set aside to be used as part of the Decor. Pour the remaining ganache into a clean mixing bowl and allow to cool and firm to the consistency of pudding. The Semisweet Chocolate Ganache can be made up to 5 days in advance and kept in an airtight container in the refrigerator, but may need to be gently reheated before using (see page 12).

CHOCOLATE CRÈME BRÛLÉE

7 ounces (1¼ cups)
64% to 70% bittersweet
chocolate, coarsely
chopped

6 large egg yolks

½ cup granulated sugar

1 cup heavy cream

1 cup whole milk

½ vanilla bean,
scraped (see page 12)

1. Preheat the oven to 250°F.

2. Melt the chocolate in a medium, heatproof mixing bowl set over a pan of simmering water (do not allow the bowl to touch the water), stirring occasionally.

3. In a separate, heatproof, nonreactive mixing bowl, whisk together the egg yolks and sugar until frothy.

4. Bring the cream, milk, and vanilla bean seeds to a boil in a medium, heavy saucepan over medium-high heat. While whisking continuously, slowly pour the warm cream over the egg mixture and whisk until well blended. Strain through a fine-mesh sieve into the warm, melted chocolate and stir gently to combine.

5. Pour the mixture into a 10-by-3-inch round cake pan (not a pan with a removable bottom) and bake for 30 minutes until set. The crème brûlée may crack and the center of the baked crème brûlée will still jiggle slightly when set.

6. When set, remove the crème brûlée from the oven and allow to cool to room temperature. Tightly wrap the crème brûlée in the pan in plastic wrap and freeze until firm, 4 to 6 hours. The Chocolate Crème Brûlée can be made up to 2 days in advance and stored in the freezer.

MILK CHOCOLATE CHANTILLY

6.5 ounces (1¼ cups)
milk chocolate, coarsely
chopped

2⅓ cups heavy cream

1. Place the chocolate in a medium, heatproof mixing bowl.

2. Bring the cream to a boil in a small, heavy saucepan over medium-high heat. Pour the hot cream over the chocolate and let sit for 5 minutes. Using a rubber spatula, stir gently in a circular motion until mixture is fully combined and homogenous.

3. Allow the mixture to cool, then cover with plastic wrap and refrigerate overnight. The Milk Chocolate Chantilly will settle while resting in the refrigerator. Milk Chocolate Chantilly can be made up to 2 days in advance and stored in an airtight container in the refrigerator. During the assembly process it will be whipped up in the mixer like whipped cream.

CHOCOLATE ALMOND PRALINE

2 tablespoons grapeseed
or vegetable oil

¼ cup whole milk

⅓ cup unsalted butter,
cubed

2 tablespoons glucose
or light corn syrup

½ cup granulated sugar

2 tablespoons cocoa powder

1 cup slivered almonds,
lightly toasted

1. Generously coat a baking sheet with the oil or line the baking sheet with a Silpat and set aside.

2. Bring the milk, butter, glucose, and sugar to a boil in a medium, heavy saucepan. Insert a candy thermometer and cook over medium-high heat until the mixture reaches 310°F, from 7 to 8 minutes. The mixture should be thick and have started to lightly color. Remove the pan from the heat and set the candy thermometer aside. Add the cocoa powder and mix well. Stir in the toasted almonds.

3. Using an offset spatula, carefully spread the hot mixture onto the prepared baking sheet and set aside to cool. The Chocolate Almond Praline is best when made within 24 hours of being used or it may become too sticky.

Chocolate Crème Brûlée

1 recipe Milk Chocolate Chantilly

Chocolate Sour Cream Cake, baked and cooled

1 recipe Cocoa Simple Syrup

1½ cups Semisweet Chocolate Ganache, softened (see page 12)

1. Remove the crème brûlée from the freezer and unmold: Run a hot knife around the inside of the pan, then with a hair dryer set on low, gently heat the bottom of the pan to release the crème brûlée (hold the pan in one hand and heat it from underneath and around the sides). Flip the loosened crème brûlée over onto a cardboard cake board. Keep in the freezer until ready to use.

2. In the bowl of a stand mixer fitted with the whisk attachment, whip the chantilly until stiff peaks form, 2 to 3 minutes, being careful to avoid over-whipping and curdling. If you underwhip the mixture, the chantilly will not hold up when you assemble the cake.

3. Place the unwrapped Chocolate Sour Cream Cake on a flat work surface. Using a long serrated knife, slice off the top ¼ inch to even out the top of the cake as necessary. Slice the cake horizontally into 3 equal layers.

4. Using a 10-inch round cake board as the bottom of a 10-by-3-inch round cake pan with removable bottom (see page 13), place 1 cake layer on the cake board, cut side up. Using a pastry brush, moisten the cake layer with one-third of the Cocoa Simple Syrup. Using an offset spatula, spread ½ cup of the ganache evenly over the syrup-soaked cake layer and cover with the frozen crème brûlée, pressing it down gently into the ganache.

5. Top with a second layer of cake and repeat with another one-third of the simple syrup and ½ cup of ganache. Using an offset spatula, spread the chantilly evenly over the ganache.

6. Top with the final layer of cake, moisten with the remaining syrup, and cover with the remaining ganache. Tightly wrap the pan in plastic and place in the freezer overnight.

DECOR

1 recipe Chocolate Almond Praline

Reserved 1¾ cups Semisweet Chocolate Ganache, softened (see page 12)

3 tablespoons powdered sugar

16 dark-chocolate-covered almonds

Caramel Sauce and Chocolate Sauce (pages 168–169) (optional)

1. Break apart the cooled Chocolate Almond Praline. In 2 separate batches, grind to a medium to fine powder in a food processor fitted with the blade attachment, leaving a few large pieces for texture.

2. Remove the assembled cake from the freezer, remove the plastic wrap, and unmold the cake from the pan (see page 14). Using an offset spatula, spread about two-thirds of the softened ganache around the sides and top of the cake as evenly as possible. Press the ground Chocolate Almond Praline evenly around the sides of the cake to completely cover the ganache and sprinkle any remaining praline over the top of the cake. Fill a small sieve with the powdered sugar and generously dust the top of the cake. Place the decorated cake on a doily-covered 12-inch round cake board or directly onto a cake plate.

3. Place the remaining Semisweet Chocolate Ganache in a pastry bag with a ¼-inch, 7 point star decorating tip and pipe 16 rosettes around the top edge of the cake to mark each slice. Top each rosette with a chocolate-covered almond. Alternatively, to create the decor as seen in the photo, refer to page 16 to make chocolate shavings.

4. Defrost the decorated cake for 4 to 6 hours in the refrigerator. Allow the cake to come to room temperature for 1 to 2 hours before serving.

Decadent Yogi

The more time I spend going inward with my yoga practice, the more I have challenged myself to create desserts that align with both my dietary desires and those of my clients. This is a rich, vegan chocolate dessert with a gluten-free option. When making desserts that are good for you, I don't compromise flavor. Even non-vegans will enjoy this cake.

To make it gluten-free, substitute 1 cup brown rice flour and 1 cup sorghum flour for the all-purpose flour. The cake will be just as moist, delicious, and flavorful thanks to the coconut flour, which also adds protein and fiber. Coconut flakes, however finely ground, are not a substitute for coconut flour and should not be used as such. The batter recipe here will yield six individual Bundt cakes or one 10-inch Bundt cake. To bake individuals, you will need a 9-by-14-by-2-inch pan that has six 1-cup Bundt cavities.

CHOCOLATE CAKES

MAKES 6 INDIVIDUAL BUNDT
CAKES OR ONE 10-INCH BUNDT
CAKE | SERVES 6

Earth Balance Vegan Butter
Stick, room temperature

2 tablespoons coconut flour

2 cups all-purpose flour

1½ teaspoons baking powder

1 teaspoon baking soda

½ teaspoon salt

2 tablespoons instant
coffee granules

⅔ cup cocoa powder, sifted

⅓ cup grapeseed
or vegetable oil

¾ cup (packed) brown sugar

¾ cup turbinado sugar

⅓ cup pureed banana
(about 1 small banana)

2 teaspoons potato starch

2 teaspoons vanilla extract

1. Preheat the oven to 300°F. Generously grease the individual cavities of a 6-cup Bundt pan or one 10-inch Bundt pan with the softened vegan butter stick.

2. Sift together both flours, the baking powder, baking soda, and salt and set aside.

3. Bring 1¾ cups water to a boil in a small, heavy saucepan over medium-high heat. Remove the pan from the heat and whisk in the instant coffee. When fully combined, whisk the coffee mixture into the sifted cocoa powder.

4. In the bowl of a stand mixer fitted with the whisk attachment, combine the oil, both sugars, banana, potato starch, and vanilla. Whip on medium speed until very well combined, 3 to 5 minutes. Remove the bowl from the mixer. Using a rubber spatula, fold in the sifted dry ingredients in 3 additions, alternating with the coffee-cocoa mixture.

5. Using a ½-cup dry measure, fill each of the 6 prepared Bundt cavities with ½ cup of batter. (If using a 10-inch Bundt pan, pour all of the batter into the prepared pan.)

6. Place the cake pan on a rack in the center of the oven and bake until an inserted knife comes out clean, about 30 minutes for the smaller cakes, 50 minutes for the 10-inch cake. The cakes should appear moist and spongy. Allow the cakes to cool completely.

7. When fully cooled, remove the cakes from the pan and wrap tightly in plastic wrap. The Chocolate Cakes can be made 1 day in advance and stored at room temperature.

CHOCOLATE FROSTING

¼ cup plus 2 tablespoons
Earth Balance
Vegan Butter Sticks,
room temperature

2¼ cups sifted
powdered sugar

¼ cup plus 2 tablespoons
sifted cocoa powder

3 tablespoons soy milk

1 teaspoon vanilla extract

1. In the bowl of a stand mixer fitted with the whisk attachment, whip the vegan butter on medium-high speed for about 3 minutes. It will appear fluffier.

2. Combine the sifted powdered sugar and cocoa powder and add to the vegan butter. Whip on medium speed for about 2 minutes. Using a rubber spatula, scrape down the sides of the bowl. Add the soy milk and vanilla and whip until well combined.

3. Remove the bowl from the mixer. Cover the bowl with plastic wrap and hold at room temperature until ready to frost the individual cakes, but for no longer than 3 hours before using.

CHOCOLATE CRUNCH

2 ounces (⅓ cup) vegan
chocolate chips

2 teaspoons grapeseed
or vegetable oil

1 cup puffed brown
rice cereal

1. Line a baking sheet with a piece of parchment paper or a Silpat and set aside.

2. Melt the vegan chocolate chips in a medium, heatproof mixing bowl set over a pan of simmering water (do not allow the bowl to touch the water), stirring occasionally. Remove from the heat, and using a rubber spatula, mix in the oil until smooth and homogenous. While the chocolate mixture is warm but not hot, fold in the cereal until well incorporated.

3. Using a metal spatula, spread the mixture as thinly as possible onto the prepared baking sheet. Place the Chocolate Crunch in the refrigerator until firm, about 15 minutes. Break up the crunch into large pieces and reserve in the refrigerator until ready to use, or for up to 4 hours.

1 recipe Chocolate Frosting

6 individual Chocolate Cakes
or 1 large cake, baked and cooled

1 recipe Chocolate Crunch

Fresh green leaves, such as
lemon, grape, or hydrangea

For the individual Bundt cakes:

1. Fit a pastry bag with a ¼-inch round decorating tip and fill with Chocolate Frosting.

2. Place the individual Bundt cakes on a platter and one by one, using the prepared pastry bag, pipe lines of frosting along the creases of the Bundt cake. Finish the center with a dollop of frosting that will hold the Chocolate Crunch pieces in place.

3. Refrigerate the decorated cakes for 2 hours to set. When ready, place frosted cakes on a serving platter and decorate with fresh green leaves from the garden.

4. Allow the decorated cakes to come to room temperature for 1 to 2 hours before serving.

For a 10-inch Bundt cake:

1. Place the cake on a 10-inch round cake board. Using an offset spatula, spread the chocolate frosting over the top of the cake to cover. Top with Chocolate Crunch pieces. Refrigerate and serve as per steps 3 and 4, above.

2. Alternatively, omit the frosting and the Chocolate Crunch. Immediately before serving, use a small sieve to dust the cake with 2 tablespoons sifted powdered sugar.

Marco Polo

Named for a signature tea from Mariage Frères, a French company that specializes in the finest tea blends, this torte reminds me of happy afternoons spent in their store in the Marais neighborhood of Paris. These teas make delicious cake and ice cream flavorings. The notes of flowers, berries, and vanilla in the Marco Polo blend give this cake a unique flavor, but if you cannot obtain it, any strongly flavored berry tea can be substituted.

To complement the light creaminess of the vanilla mousse, I add fresh blackberries and a tart blackberry glaze (what the French call a *miroir* because of its reflective surface). A miroir combines a fruit puree and gelatin to create a colorful, fruit-forward finish. The delightfully crunchy streusel imparts textural contrast. For a less formal look, finish the cake with fresh berries; for a dramatic and bold effect, top the glaze with fresh flowers.

When assembling the dessert, cut the joconde (a type of cake containing almond flour) very thinly so that all the layers will stack properly in the cake pan. The vanilla mousse is best made the same day the cake is assembled, to prevent it from firming up too much in the refrigerator. Likewise, the Marco Polo Streusel should be made the day you decorate the cake. If you prefer to omit this step, simply toast and grind any leftover cake pieces and use the crumbs to edge the sides.

MARCO POLO VANILLA JOCONDE CAKE

SERVES 12 TO 14

2 teaspoons unsalted butter, melted but not hot

3 teaspoons loose-leaf Mariage Frères Marco Polo tea

1 cup all-purpose flour

1 cup plus 2 tablespoons powdered sugar, sifted

1½ cups almond flour

2 large eggs

5 large egg yolks

6 large egg whites

¼ cup plus 2 tablespoons granulated sugar

1. Preheat the oven to 300°F. Grease the bottom and sides of a 10-by-3-inch round cake pan with removable bottom with the melted butter and line the bottom with a 10-inch-diameter parchment paper round.

2. Grind the tea in a coffee or spice grinder to a powder. Sift together the all-purpose flour and powdered sugar and place into the bowl of a food processor fitted with the blade attachment. Add the almond flour and ground tea and process to a finely ground powder. Set aside.

3. In the bowl of a stand mixer fitted with the whisk attachment, whip together the whole eggs and egg yolks on medium-high speed until light in color and thick in volume, about 3 minutes. Increase the mixer speed to high and whip for another 3 minutes.

4. Reduce the mixer speed to low and add the freshly processed flour mixture to the eggs, mixing just until combined, being careful not to overbeat. Transfer the batter to a clean mixing bowl large enough to mix in the meringue (see step 6).

5. In the bowl of a stand mixer fitted with the whisk attachment, whip the egg whites on medium speed for 2 minutes. When the egg whites are frothy, begin to slowly add the granulated sugar and increase the mixer speed to medium-high. Whip until the egg whites are stiff with a creamy texture, about 5 minutes. Remove the bowl from the mixer.

6. Using a rubber spatula, carefully fold the meringue into the cake batter in 3 additions until fully combined.

7. Pour the batter into the prepared cake pan and place on a rack in the center of the oven. Bake the cake until a knife inserted into the center comes out clean, about 50 minutes. The cake will have a slightly golden color and a spongelike texture.

8. Remove the cake from the oven and allow to cool completely. Once cooled, remove the cake from the pan (see page 12) and peel the parchment paper from the bottom of the cake. Wrap the cake tightly in plastic wrap until ready to use. The Marco Polo Vanilla Joconde Cake can be stored for up to 1 day in the refrigerator or in the freezer for up to 1 week.

MARCO POLO SIMPLE SYRUP

1 cup granulated sugar

3 teaspoons loose-leaf Mariage Frères Marco Polo tea

1 teaspoon vanilla extract

1. Combine the sugar with 1 cup water in a small, heavy saucepan over medium-high heat and bring to a boil, stirring occasionally. Remove from the heat and stir in the tea until blended. Allow to steep for 4 minutes. Strain the syrup through a fine-mesh sieve into a clean bowl and allow to cool.

2. Once fully cooled, stir in ¼ cup water and the vanilla extract until combined. The Marco Polo Simple Syrup will keep for up to 3 days in an airtight container in the refrigerator.

VANILLA BEAN MOUSSE

6 gelatin sheets (see page 11)

2 cups whole milk

2 whole vanilla beans, scraped (see page 12)

8 large egg yolks

½ cup granulated sugar

1¾ cups heavy cream

1. Soften the gelatin sheets in 6 cups cool water for 5 minutes.

2. Bring the milk and vanilla bean seeds to a boil in a medium, heavy saucepan over medium-high heat.

3. Whisk together the egg yolks and sugar in a heatproof, nonreactive mixing bowl until frothy. While whisking continuously, slowly pour the hot milk into the egg yolk mixture in several additions, incorporating fully after each addition.

4. Pour the mixture back into the saucepan and continue to cook over medium heat, whisking continuously, until the mixture begins to boil and has thickened to a custard. Strain through a fine-mesh sieve into a clean bowl.

5. Squeeze the excess water from the softened gelatin and mix the gelatin into the warm custard until fully dissolved and the custard is smooth. Cover with plastic wrap and place the custard in the refrigerator for 45 minutes to cool.

6. Once the custard has cooled, in the bowl of a stand mixer fitted with the whisk attachment, whip the heavy cream until soft peaks form, 1 to 2 minutes. Using a rubber spatula, gently fold the whipped cream into the custard in several additions until fully combined and creamy. The Vanilla Bean Mousse should be made when ready to assemble the cake.

ASSEMBLY

1 recipe Vanilla Bean Mousse

1 pint fresh blackberries, halved lengthwise

2 cups heavy cream

3 tablespoons granulated sugar

Marco Polo Vanilla Joconde Cake, baked and cooled

1 recipe Marco Polo Simple Syrup

1. Reserve 1 cup of the Vanilla Bean Mousse and set aside.

2. Combine the cream and sugar in the bowl of a stand mixer fitted with the whisk attachment and whip until stiff peaks form, 2 minutes. Fit a pastry bag with a ½-inch, plain round decorating tip and fill with all of the whipped cream.

3. Unwrap the joconde and place it on a flat work surface. Using a long serrated knife, slice off the top ¼ inch to even out the top as necessary. Slice the cake horizontally into three ¼-inch-thick layers.

4. Using a 10-inch round cake board as the bottom of a 10-by-3-inch round cake pan with removable bottom (see page 13), place 1 cake layer on the cake board, cut side up. Using a pastry brush, moisten the cake layer with one-third of the Marco Polo Simple Syrup.

5. Using an offset spatula, spread 2½ cups of Vanilla Bean Mousse evenly onto the syrup-soaked cake layer and top with half of the blackberry slices. Using the filled pastry bag, cover with a piped layer of whipped cream.

6. Top with a second layer of cake and repeat with the syrup, mousse, remaining blackberries, and the rest of the whipped cream.

7. Top with the final layer of cake, moisten with the remaining syrup, and cover with the reserved 1 cup Vanilla Bean Mousse, spreading the mousse as evenly as possible across the surface of the cake.

8. Tightly wrap the cake in the pan in plastic wrap and place in the freezer overnight.

MARCO POLO STREUSEL

½ cup unsalted butter, very cold, cut into ¼-inch cubes, plus 2 teaspoons, melted but not hot, for greasing sheet

3 teaspoons loose-leaf Mariage Frères Marco Polo tea

⅓ cup all-purpose flour

⅓ cup powdered sugar, sifted

⅓ cup plus 2 tablespoons almond flour

½ teaspoon salt

1. Preheat the oven to 300°F. Lightly grease a baking sheet with 2 teaspoons melted butter or line with a Silpat and set aside.

2. Grind the tea in a coffee or spice grinder to a powder. Sift together the all-purpose flour and powdered sugar into the bowl of a food processor fitted with the blade attachment. Add the almond flour, salt, and ground tea and pulse to a finely ground powder.

3. Add the cubed butter in several additions, pulsing lightly after each addition, until the dough is crumbly.

4. Crumble the streusel onto the prepared baking sheet and place on a rack in the center of the oven. Bake until the streusel colors slightly and hardens to a shortbread consistency, about 15 minutes.

5. Remove the streusel from the oven and allow to cool completely before chopping it into small pieces. The Marco Polo Streusel should be made when ready to decorate the cake.

1 (8-ounce) bag frozen
blackberries, thawed

3 gelatin sheets (see page 11)

⅓ cup granulated sugar

3 tablespoons glucose
or light corn syrup

⅓ cup blackberry
or raspberry jam, strained

1. In the bowl of a food processor fitted with the blade attachment, process 1 cup of the thawed blackberries until pureed. You should have ½ cup puree.

2. Soften the gelatin sheets in 3 cups of cool water for 5 minutes.

3. Pour the puree into a small, heavy saucepan and add the sugar, glucose, and jam. Place over medium-high heat and bring to a boil. Once the mixture boils, insert a candy thermometer and stir continuously until the mixture reaches 220°F, about 5 minutes.

4. Remove the pan from the heat. Squeeze the excess water from the gelatin sheets and stir into the hot mixture. Place back over medium-high heat and cook, stirring for 2 minutes. Strain into a clean bowl and allow the Blackberry Miroir to cool slightly. The Blackberry Miroir should be made when ready to use.

DECOR

1 recipe Blackberry Mirroir

1 recipe Marco Polo Streusel,
cooled and finely chopped

1 pint fresh blackberries
or fresh flowers (optional)

Blackberry Sauce and Vanilla
Sauce (pages 168 and 170)
(optional)

1. Remove the assembled cake from the freezer, remove the plastic wrap, and pour the hot Blackberry Miroir onto the top of the cake. Quickly swirl the cake pan around until the mirroir completely covers the top of the entire cake. If the mirroir has dripped down the outside of the cake pan, wipe it off with a wet towel so that the outside of the cake pan is very clean, thus avoiding a potentially sticky mess in your freezer.

2. Return the cake to the freezer for 1 hour to allow the mirroir to fully set. When ready, unmold the cake from the pan (see page 14). Allow the cake to defrost in the refrigerator, uncovered, for a minimum of 8 hours or overnight.

3. When ready to serve, remove the glazed cake from the refrigerator and press the Marco Polo Streusel crumbs evenly and completely around the sides of the cake (see page 14). Transfer the decorated cake to a serving platter or doily-covered 12-inch round cake board. If desired, decorate the top with fresh blackberries or flowers and serve with sauce.

Extraordinary
SUMMER

Passion Fruit Ricotta Cake

Travel is both my passion and a great source of inspiration. One winter when I was studying in France, I found my-self craving the tropics, and this homesickness for the sun (I grew up in the endless summer of San Diego) gave birth to the Passion Fruit Ricotta Cake. Delightfully sophisticated and richly fruity, this is a huge crowd-pleaser that tastes like pure summer sunshine and is perfect for any gathering.

You'll need to make two batches of the Passion Fruit Whipped Cream to assemble the cake. Because the acid in the passion fruit puree (see page 11) quickly breaks down the whipped cream, prepare each batch separately and use immediately as specified by the recipe.

RICOTTA POUND CAKE

MAKES ONE 10-INCH CAKE

SERVES 14 TO 16

2 teaspoons unsalted butter, melted but not hot

6 large eggs

2 cups granulated sugar

1 cup grapeseed or vegetable oil

1 cup whole or skim-milk ricotta

1 teaspoon freshly squeezed lemon juice

½ teaspoon vanilla extract

3 cups all-purpose flour

3 teaspoons baking powder

1. Preheat the oven to 300°F. Grease the bottom and sides of a 10-by-3-inch round cake pan with a removable bottom with the melted butter and line the bottom with a 10-inch-diameter parchment paper round.

2. In the bowl of a stand mixer fitted with the whisk attachment, whip together the eggs and sugar at medium-high speed until the mixture is very thick and falls in heavy ribbons, about 7 minutes.

3. In a separate bowl, whisk together the oil, ricotta, lemon juice, and vanilla. Gently add the ricotta mixture to the egg mixture and whip just until blended.

4. Sift together the flour and baking powder. Add the sifted ingredients to the batter, mixing just until incorporated, scraping down the sides of the mixing bowl as needed. Do not overmix. If necessary, finish folding in the sifted ingredients by hand, using a rubber spatula.

5. Pour the batter into the prepared cake pan and place on a rack in the center of the oven. Bake the cake until golden brown, about 90 minutes. The cake is done when a knife blade inserted in the center comes out clean and when the top of the cake springs back lightly when touched.

6. Remove the cake from the oven and allow to cool completely. Once cooled, remove the cake from the pan (see page 12) and peel the parchment paper from the bottom of the cake. Wrap the cake tightly in plastic wrap until ready to use. The Ricotta Pound Cake can be stored for up to 1 day at room temperature or in the freezer for up to 1 week.

PASSION FRUIT SIMPLE SYRUP

½ cup granulated sugar

¾ cup passion fruit puree

1. Combine the sugar with ½ cup water in a small, heavy saucepan over medium-high heat and bring to a boil, stirring occasionally. Remove from the heat, pour into a clean bowl, and allow to cool.

2. Once fully cooled, stir in the passion fruit puree until combined. The Passion Fruit Simple Syrup will keep for up to 2 days in an airtight container in the refrigerator.

PASSION FRUIT CURD

2 gelatin sheets (see page 11)

4 large eggs

¾ cup passion fruit puree

¾ cup plus 1 tablespoon granulated sugar

1½ tablespoons freshly squeezed lemon juice

1½ cups unsalted butter, room temperature, cut into ¼-inch cubes

1. Soften the gelatin sheets in 2 cups cool water for 5 minutes.

2. Combine the eggs, puree, sugar, and lemon juice in a heatproof, nonreactive mixing bowl over a saucepan of simmering water (do not allow the bowl to touch the water) and whisk together until the sugar begins to dissolve. Cook, whisking continuously, until the mixture begins to thicken to a custard, 5 to 7 minutes. Whisk in the butter. The curd should be smooth and homogenous.

3. Squeeze out the excess water from the softened gelatin and whisk the gelatin into the hot mixture until fully dissolved and combined.

4. Remove the bowl from over the water and strain the curd through a medium-mesh sieve into a clean, nonreactive mixing bowl. Cover with plastic wrap pressed directly onto the surface of the curd and allow to cool. The Passion Fruit Curd can be kept for up to 5 days in an airtight container in the refrigerator.

PASSION FRUIT WHIPPED CREAM

2 cups heavy cream

2 tablespoons granulated sugar

½ recipe Passion Fruit Curd

In the bowl of a stand mixer fitted with the whisk attachment, whip together the cream and sugar until stiff peaks form, about 2 minutes. Remove the bowl from the mixer. Using a rubber spatula, fold the whipped cream into the Passion Fruit Curd until combined. The Passion Fruit Whipped Cream must be made when ready to use.

ASSEMBLY

1 pint fresh strawberries

2 ripe medium to large
kiwi fruits, peeled

1 ripe medium banana

Ricotta Pound Cake,
baked and cooled

1 recipe Passion Fruit
Simple Syrup

1 recipe Passion Fruit
Whipped Cream

1. Set aside 3 strawberries to be used for Decor. Hull the remaining strawberries (about 1 cup) and cut each lengthwise into 4 slices. Slice the kiwi into six ½-inch-thick rounds and set 2 rounds aside. Cut the remaining rounds into quarters. Peel the banana and slice into ⅛-inch rounds. Cut each round in half.

2. Place the unwrapped pound cake on a flat work surface. Using a long serrated knife, slice off the top ¼ inch to even out the top of the cake as necessary. Set cut piece aside to be used later as an option to edge the cake (see page 14). Slice the cake horizontally into 3 even layers.

3. Using a 10-inch round cake board as the bottom of a 10-by-3-inch round cake pan with removable bottom (see page 13), place 1 cake layer on the cake board, cut side up. Using a pastry brush, moisten the cake layer with one-third of the Passion Fruit Simple Syrup.

4. Using an offset spatula, spread half of the Passion Fruit Whipped Cream onto the syrup-soaked cake layer and sprinkle evenly with the kiwi and banana slices.

5. Top with the second layer of pound cake and repeat with one-third of the syrup and the remaining whipped cream. Sprinkle evenly with all of the sliced strawberries.

6. Top with the final layer of cake and moisten with the remaining syrup. Tightly wrap the pan in plastic and place in the freezer overnight.

DECOR

1 recipe Passion Fruit
Whipped Cream

Toasted cake crumbs
(see page 14)

Reserved 3 whole strawberries,
stems attached

1 fresh passion fruit (optional)

2 to 3 fresh roses or
flower petals (optional)

Passion Fruit and Kiwi
or Raspberry Sauce
(pages 169–170) (optional)

1. Remove the cake from the freezer, remove the plastic wrap, and unmold the cake from the pan (see page 14). Using an offset spatula, evenly spread half of the Passion Fruit Whipped Cream around the sides and top of the cake. Press the toasted cake crumbs evenly onto the sides of the cake to completely cover the whipped cream (see page 15).

2. Fit a pastry bag with a ½-inch round decorating tip and fill with the remaining Passion Fruit Whipped Cream. Pipe 3-inch-long curved lines in concentric circles over the top of the cake, from the outside edge working toward the center, to completely cover. Place the decorated cake in the refrigerator overnight to defrost and to allow the fruit inside the cake to thaw fully.

3. When ready to serve, remove the cake from the refrigerator and decorate the top of the cake with the strawberries and the optional passion fruit and fresh flowers if desired. Place the cake on a doily-covered 12-inch round cake board or directly onto a cake plate and serve cold, with sauce if desired.

Beau Soleil

Just one bite of Beau Soleil transports me back to a picnic in Aix-en-Provence on a warm summer day, when we enjoyed ripe juicy peaches near the beach. In addition to peach curd, I fill this cake with other sunny Mediterranean flavors, including honey, hazelnut praline, and mascarpone cheese. It lacks nothing—other than a sweet dessert wine and a one-way ticket to the South of France.

For this recipe, I prefer a mild floral honey, which provides just the right accent. The Peach Curd is best when made the same day as assembling the cake, especially if using the gelatin, which will firm up too much when chilled. If omitting the gelatin, the Peach Curd can be covered with plastic wrap and stored for up to 1 day in the refrigerator.

HAZELNUT VANILLA JOCONDE

MAKES ONE 10-INCH CAKE

SERVES 14 TO 16

¼ cup unsalted butter, melted but not hot, plus 2 teaspoons, for greasing pan

2 large eggs

6 large egg yolks

¾ cup granulated sugar

1 tablespoon honey

1⅓ cups almond flour

1 cup all-purpose flour

½ cup hazelnuts, skinned, lightly toasted and cooled

5 large egg whites

1. Preheat the oven to 325°F. Grease the bottom and sides of a 10-by-3-inch round cake pan with removable bottom with 2 teaspoons of the melted butter and line the bottom with a 10-inch-diameter parchment paper round.

2. In the bowl of a stand mixer fitted with the whisk attachment, whip together the whole eggs and egg yolks with ½ cup of the sugar on medium-high speed until light in color and thick, about 5 minutes. Add the honey and whip for 2 minutes. The batter will continue to thicken and lighten in color.

3. While the eggs are whipping, combine both flours and the hazelnuts in the bowl of a food processor fitted with the blade attachment. Process until the mixture is finely ground.

4. Reduce the mixer speed to low and add the freshly processed mixture to the whipping eggs, being careful not to overmix the batter. Transfer the batter to a clean mixing bowl large enough to mix in the meringue (see step 6).

5. In the bowl of a stand mixer fitted with the whisk attachment, whip the egg whites on medium speed for 2 minutes. When the egg whites are frothy, slowly add the remaining ¼ cup sugar and increase the speed to medium-high. Whip until the egg whites are stiff with a creamy texture, about 3 minutes.

6. Using a rubber spatula, carefully fold half of the meringue and then half of the ¼ cup melted butter into the batter. Repeat with the remaining meringue and melted butter. Pour the batter into the prepared cake pan and place on a rack in the center of the oven. Bake until a knife inserted into the center comes out clean, about 40 minutes. The cake will be slightly golden, with a nutty, spongelike texture.

7. Remove the cake from the oven and allow to cool completely. Once cooled, remove the cake from the pan (see page 12) and peel the parchment paper from the bottom of the cake. Wrap the cake tightly in plastic wrap until ready to use. The Hazelnut Vanilla Joconde can be stored for up to 1 day at room temperature or in the freezer for up to 1 week.

ORANGE SIMPLE SYRUP

½ cup granulated sugar

Grated zest of
1 medium orange

Juice of 1 medium
orange, strained

1 teaspoon freshly
squeezed lemon juice,
strained

1. Combine the sugar, zest, and ½ cup water in a small, heavy saucepan over medium-high heat and bring to a boil, stirring occasionally. Remove from the heat. Pour into a clean bowl and allow to cool.

2. Once fully cooled, strain the syrup into a clean container and stir in the two juices. The Orange Simple Syrup will keep for up to 1 day in an airtight container in the refrigerator. However, the flavor might change if stored for a longer period of time.

MASCARPONE MOUSSE

½ cup heavy cream

⅔ cup granulated sugar

7 large egg yolks

1 whole vanilla bean,
scraped (see page 12)

4 gelatin sheets
(see page 11)

1 (17.6-ounce/500 g)
container mascarpone
cheese, room temperature

1. In the bowl of a stand mixer fitted with the whisk attachment, whip the cream until soft peaks form, about 1 minute. Hold in the refrigerator until ready to use.

2. Combine the sugar with ¼ cup water in a small, heavy saucepan and bring to a boil over medium heat. Insert a candy thermometer and cook until the temperature reaches 230° to 240°F, the soft-ball stage.

3. While the sugar is cooking, combine the egg yolks and vanilla bean seeds in the bowl of a stand mixer fitted with the whisk attachment and whip at medium-high speed until light and thick, about 3 minutes.

4. Carefully pour the hot sugar into the whipping yolks in a continuous stream, being careful to avoid pouring the hot syrup directly onto the moving whisk. Increase the mixer speed to high and whip until mixture has cooled down and has tripled in volume, 7 to 10 minutes.

5. While the egg yolks are whipping, soften the gelatin sheets in 4 cups cool water for 5 minutes. Squeeze out the excess water, then melt the gelatin in a small saucepan over low heat until liquid. Add to the whipping egg mixture and whip until the gelatin is completely dissolved and incorporated. Remove the bowl from the mixer.

6. Place the mascarpone in a medium mixing bowl and whisk to loosen. If the cheese is too cold, warm it up very gently in the microwave just to soften. Using a rubber spatula, fold the mascarpone into the cooled egg mixture in several additions. The mixture should be smooth and creamy after each addition.

7. Using a rubber spatula, gently fold in the whipped cream. Cover with plastic wrap and hold at room temperature until ready to use, but for no longer than 1 hour. The Mascarpone Mousse should be made when you are ready to assemble the cake due to the addition of gelatin. The gelatin firms up rather quickly and you risk getting a lumpy mousse if you have to reheat it to soften.

3⅛ cups frozen peaches, or
5 to 6 large fresh peaches,
peeled and pitted

2 tablespoons unsalted
butter, room temperature

3 tablespoons tightly
packed brown sugar

1 whole vanilla bean,
scraped (see page 12)

½ teaspoon ground
cardamom

½ teaspoon ground ginger

¼ teaspoon ground cinnamon

2 gelatin sheets (see page 11)
(optional)

5 tablespoons granulated
sugar

2 tablespoons cornstarch

1. If you are using frozen peaches, thaw them to room temperature. Cut ⅔ cup frozen peaches or 1 fresh peach into ¼-inch cubes.

2. Combine the butter, brown sugar, vanilla bean seeds, and all the spices in a medium, nonstick sauté pan over medium-high heat. Cook until the butter has completely melted. Add the diced peaches and cook, stirring continuously, until the peaches have softened and caramelized, about 5 minutes. Remove from the heat, transfer to a clean mixing bowl, and allow to cool. If using gelatin, soften the gelatin sheets in 2 cups cool water for 5 minutes. Squeeze out the excess water and stir the gelatin into the warm peaches until melted and dissolved. Set aside.

3. In the bowl of a food processor fitted with the blade attachment, combine the remaining frozen or fresh peaches with half of the granulated sugar. Process the peaches to a chunky puree and transfer to a medium, heavy saucepan. Combine the remaining granulated sugar with the cornstarch and add to the puree in the saucepan, mixing until well combined.

4. Place the saucepan over medium heat and cook until the puree begins to boil and thicken, 4 to 5 minutes. Remove the pan from the heat and add the caramelized peaches. Gently stir until very well combined. Transfer the mixture to a clean bowl and allow to cool at room temperature for 1 hour before using.

1 cup granulated sugar

1½ cup hazelnuts,
skinned and lightly toasted

1. Line a baking sheet with parchment paper or a Silpat and set aside.

2. In a medium, heavy saucepan, bring the sugar and ⅓ cup water to a rolling boil over medium heat. Using a heat-resistant rubber spatula, stir in the hazelnuts. Mix continuously until the cooked sugar coats the nuts in a sandlike consistency, about 5 minutes. Continue to mix and cook until the nuts become glossy and take on a caramelized color, 2 to 3 minutes.

3. Using an offset spatula, carefully spread the hot mixture onto the prepared baking sheet and allow to cool for about 30 minutes.

4. When fully cooled, grind in a food processor fitted with the blade attachment to the desired consistency. More finely ground praline will lend a more elegant appearance to the finished caked. The Hazelnut Praline will be used in both the assembly and Decor of the cake.

5. The Hazelnut Praline can be made up to 2 days in advance and stored in an airtight container. However, it is preferable to use it within 24 hours of preparation.

ASSEMBLY

1 recipe Mascarpone Mousse

1½ cups heavy cream

2 tablespoons granulated sugar

Hazelnut Vanilla Joconde,
baked and cooled

1 recipe Orange Simple Syrup

1 recipe Peach Curd

2 tablespoons honey

⅔ cup Hazelnut Praline

1. Measure out 1 cup of Mascarpone Mousse and set aside to be used on the top layer of the cake.

2. In the bowl of a stand mixer fitted with the whisk attachment, whip together the cream and sugar until stiff peaks form, 1 to 2 minutes. Fit a pastry bag with a ½-inch plain round decorating tip and fill with all of the whipped cream. Hold in the refrigerator until ready to use.

3. Place the unwrapped joconde on a flat work surface. Using a long serrated knife, slice off the top ¼ inch to even out the top of the cake as necessary. Slice the cake horizontally into three ¼-inch-thick layers.

4. Using a 10-inch round cake board as the bottom of a 10-by-3-inch round cake pan with removable bottom (see page 13), place 1 cake layer on the cake board, cut side up. Using a pastry brush, moisten the cake layer with one-third of the Orange Simple Syrup.

5. Using an offset spatula, spread half of the remaining Mascarpone Mousse evenly onto the syrup-soaked cake layer and cover with approximately half of the Peach Curd. Using the prepared pastry bag, pipe approximately half of the whipped cream on top of the curd in a spiral pattern. Drizzle with 1 tablespoon honey and cover with approximately ⅓ cup of the Hazelnut Praline.

6. Top with the second layer of joconde and repeat with one-third of the syrup, the remaining mousse, remaining curd, remaining whipped cream, 1 tablespoon honey, and remaining ⅓ cup praline.

7. Top with the final layer of cake and moisten with the remaining Orange Simple Syrup. Spread the reserved 1 cup Mascarpone Mousse as evenly and as smoothly as possible over the top of the cake. Tightly wrap the cake in the pan in plastic wrap and place in the freezer overnight.

DECOR

2 cups heavy cream

¼ cup granulated sugar

About ¾ cup Hazelnut Praline

5 medium fresh peaches, halved, pitted, and sliced into ⅛-inch-thick slices

Tropical Fruit and Vanilla or Raspberry Sauce (page 170) (optional)

1. In the bowl of a stand mixer fitted with the whisk attachment, whip together the cream and sugar until stiff peaks form, about 2 minutes.

2. Remove the assembled cake from the freezer, remove the plastic wrap, and unmold the cake from the pan (see page 14). Using an offset spatula, spread a thick layer of whipped cream over the top and sides of the cake as evenly as possible. Use a long metal spatula to evenly spread the whipped cream over the top so that it is nice and flat. Press the Hazelnut Praline evenly onto the sides of the cake to completely cover the whipped cream (see page 14).

3. Starting from the outside edge of the cake and working toward the center, lay peach slices in overlapping concentric circles over the top of the cake.

4. Place the decorated cake on a doily-covered, 12-inch round cake board or directly onto a cake plate. Place in the refrigerator overnight to allow the cake to fully thaw. Allow the cake to sit at room temperature for 1 hour before serving. Serve with sauce, if desired.

Diamond Head

Inspired by a visit to the beachside estate of Doris Duke near Diamond Head in Honolulu, this cake is chock-full of macadamia nuts, just like the trees that grow around the property. Semisweet chocolate balances the rich, unctuous nuts, and the génoise base provides the perfect flavor and texture to support generous quantities of cream and custard. Ground macadamia brittle, sprinkled between the layers and around the edges, imparts both complex caramel notes and a crunch that brightens this very creamy dessert. Whenever I taste Diamond Head, I recall the pleasures of visiting Hawaii.

BITTERSWEET CHOCOLATE GÉNOISE

MAKES ONE 10-INCH CAKE

SERVES 14 TO 16

⅓ cup unsalted butter, melted and warm, plus 2 teaspoons, melted but not hot, for greasing pan

8 large eggs

¾ cup granulated sugar

¾ cup all-purpose flour

⅓ cup cocoa powder

1. Preheat the oven to 325°F. Grease the bottom and sides of a 10-by-3-inch round cake pan with removable bottom with the 2 teaspoons melted butter and line the bottom with a 10-inch-diameter parchment paper round.

2. Combine the eggs and sugar in a heatproof, nonreactive mixing bowl set over a saucepan of simmering water (do not allow the bowl to touch the water). Whisk continuously until the mixture is warm to the touch and frothy, about 4 minutes.

3. Remove the bowl from over the water and transfer to a stand mixer fitted with the whisk attachment. Whip the mixture on high speed until light in color and tripled in volume, 7 to 10 minutes. Remove the bowl from the mixer.

4. Sift together the flour and cocoa powder. Using a rubber spatula, gently fold the sifted ingredients into the cooled batter in several additions.

5. Pour the ⅓ cup melted, warm butter into a mixing bowl. Fold approximately one-third of the batter into the butter until incorporated. Gently fold this mixture back into the remaining batter, being careful not to deflate the batter. Fold just until incorporated.

6. Pour the batter into the prepared cake pan and place on a rack in the center of the oven. Bake until the cake begins to pull away slightly from the sides of the pan and springs back slightly when pressed, 30 to 35 minutes.

7. Remove the cake from the oven and allow to cool completely. Once cooled, remove the cake from the pan (see page 12) and peel the parchment paper from the bottom of the cake. Wrap the cake tightly in plastic wrap until ready to use. The Bittersweet Chocolate Génoise can be made 1 day in advance and stored at room temperature.

RUM SIMPLE SYRUP

¾ cup granulated sugar

⅓ cup Myer's dark rum

1. Combine the sugar with 1 cup water in a small, heavy saucepan over medium-high heat and bring to a boil, stirring occasionally. Remove from the heat, pour into a clean bowl, and allow to cool.

2. Once fully cooled, stir in the rum and ¼ cup water until combined. The Rum Simple Syrup will keep for up to 2 days in an airtight container in the refrigerator.

SEMISWEET CHOCOLATE GANACHE

(see page 42)

VANILLA BEAN CUSTARD

4 cups heavy cream

1½ cups whole milk

1 whole vanilla bean, scraped (see page 12)

⅔ cup granulated sugar

8 large egg yolks

3 tablespoons cornstarch

3 tablespoons potato starch

½ cup plus 2 tablespoons unsalted butter, room temperature

6 gelatin sheets (see page 11)

2 tablespoons Myer's dark rum

1. Combine 2 cups heavy cream, the milk, and vanilla bean seeds in a medium, heavy saucepan over medium-high heat and bring to a boil.

2. In a heatproof, nonreactive mixing bowl, whisk together the sugar, egg yolks, and both starches until well combined and smooth. While whisking continuously, slowly pour the warm cream mixture over the egg mixture and whisk until blended. Return all to the saucepan and continue to cook over medium heat, whisking continuously, until the mixture begins to boil and has thickened into a custard, about 5 minutes.

3. Strain the custard through a fine-mesh sieve into a clean mixing bowl and whisk in 2 tablespoons butter until smooth and fully combined. Cover with plastic wrap pressed directly onto the surface of the custard and cool in the refrigerator for 2 hours.

4. Once the custard has cooled and is ready to use, remove it from the refrigerator.

5. In the bowl of a stand mixer fitted with the whisk attachment, whip the remaining 2 cups heavy cream until soft peaks form, about 2 minutes. Hold in the refrigerator until ready to use.

6. Soften the gelatin sheets in 6 cups cool water for 5 minutes. Squeeze out the excess water, then melt the gelatin in a small saucepan over low heat until liquid.

7. In the bowl of a stand mixer fitted with either the whisk or the paddle attachment, add the cooled custard and beat slightly to loosen. Add the remaining ½ cup butter and beat until combined. While the machine is running, pour in the melted gelatin and mix until fully incorporated and smooth. Remove the bowl from the mixer. Using a rubber spatula, gently fold in the whipped cream until just combined, then fold in the rum. The Vanilla Bean Custard should not be made more than 1 hour before ready to use and should be stored, covered with plastic wrap pressed directly onto the surface of the custard, in the refrigerator until ready to use.

2 tablespoons vegetable oil

⅓ cup granulated sugar

⅔ cup macadamia pieces

1. Generously coat a baking sheet with the oil or line a baking sheet with a Silpat and set aside.

2. In a medium, heavy saucepan, bring the sugar and 2 tablespoons water to a boil over medium heat. Using a heat-resistant rubber spatula, stir in the macadamia nuts. Mix continuously until the cooked sugar coats the nuts in a sandlike consistency. Continue to mix and cook until the nuts become glossy and take on a caramelized color, 1 to 2 minutes.

3. Using an offset spatula, carefully spread the hot mixture onto the prepared baking sheet and set aside to cool. When fully cooled, use a knife to chop the brittle into small pieces.

4. The Macadamia Brittle can be made up to 1 day in advance and stored in an airtight container. One-third cup chopped Macadamia Brittle will be used while assembling the cake, and the remaining brittle will be ground in a food processor to the desired consistency and used to finish the edges of the entire cake in the Decor portion. It is important to note that you should crush only the amount of brittle that you will need when you are ready to use it or it will become too sticky to work with.

ASSEMBLY

¾ cup macadamia nuts, lightly toasted and cooled

3 cups heavy cream

¼ cup granulated sugar

Bittersweet Chocolate Génoise, baked and cooled

1 recipe Rum Simple Syrup

1 recipe Semisweet Chocolate Ganache

1 recipe Vanilla Bean Custard

⅓ cup chopped Macadamia Brittle

1. Set aside 16 whole macadamia nuts to be used in the Decor section of the recipe and grind the remainder in a food processor fitted with the blade attachment so that the nuts are finely ground but not too oily.

2. In the bowl of a stand mixer fitted with the whisk attachment, whip together the cream and sugar until stiff peaks form, 2 to 3 minutes. Fit a pastry bag with a ½-inch plain round decorating tip and fill with half of the whipped cream. Hold all in the refrigerator until ready to use.

3. Place the unwrapped génoise on a flat work surface. Using a long serrated knife, slice off the top ¼ inch to even out the top of the cake as necessary. Slice the cake horizontally into 3 even layers.

4. Using a 10-inch round cake board as the bottom of a 10-by-3-inch round cake pan with removable bottom (see page 13), place 1 cake layer on the cake board, cut side up. Using a pastry brush, moisten the cake layer with one-third of the Rum Simple Syrup.

5. Measure out 1¾ cups of the Semisweet Chocolate Ganache and set aside for use in the Decor portion. As necessary, gently reheat the remaining ganache until softened (see page 12). Using an offset spatula, spread a very thin layer of warmed Semisweet Chocolate Ganache evenly over the syrup-soaked layer and to the edge of the pan. Cover with approximately half of the Vanilla Bean Custard and sprinkle evenly with half of the chopped Macadamia Brittle and half

of the ground macadamia nuts. Using the entire filled pastry bag, pipe a layer of whipped cream over the nuts. Refill the bag with the remaining whipped cream to be used on the next layer.

6. Top with a second layer of génoise and repeat with one-third of the syrup, ganache, custard, remaining chopped Macadamia Brittle, remaining ground macadamia nuts, and the rest of the whipped cream.

7. Top with the final layer of cake and moisten with the remaining Rum Simple Syrup. Cover with a final layer of Semisweet Chocolate Ganache. Tightly wrap the cake in the pan in plastic wrap and place in the freezer overnight.

DECOR

6 ounces (1 cup) semisweet chocolate chips

½ cup heavy cream

1 teaspoon Myer's dark rum

Remaining Macadamia Brittle, finely ground

Reserved 1¾ cups Semisweet Chocolate Ganache

16 reserved toasted and cooled macadamia nuts

Chocolate Sauce, Vanilla Sauce, or Caramel Sauce (see pages 168–170) (optional)

1. Place the chocolate chips in a medium, heatproof bowl.

2. Bring the cream to a boil in a small, heavy saucepan over medium-high heat. Pour the hot cream over the chocolate chips and let sit for 5 minutes. Using a rubber spatula, stir slowly and gently in a circular motion until the mixture is fully combined and homogenous.

3. Transfer the chocolate mixture to a food processor; add the rum and process to blend (or, using an immersion blender, add the rum to the bowl with the chocolate and cream and blend to emulsify). The ganache should be thick and shiny.

4. Remove the assembled cake from the freezer, remove the plastic wrap, and unmold the cake from the pan (see page 14). Using an 11- or 12-inch-long straight spatula, spread the freshly made ganache evenly over the top and around the sides of the cake. Press the ground Macadamia Brittle evenly around the sides of the cake to cover the ganache.

5. Fit a pastry bag with a ¼-inch, 7-point star decorating tip and fill with the reserved Semisweet Chocolate Ganache. Pipe 16 rosettes around the top edge of the cake to mark each slice and top each rosette with a toasted macadamia nut.

6. Place the decorated cake on a doily-covered 12-inch round cake board or directly on a cake plate. If there is any remaining ground Macadamia Brittle, sprinkle it over the top of the cake.

7. Defrost the decorated cake in the refrigerator for 8 hours or overnight. The cake can be displayed at room temperature for up to 1 hour before serving. Serve slices with sauce, if desired.

Chocolate Nirvana

When I truly need to recharge and relax, I head to Bali, which to me is Nirvana. I always find myself receptive to new flavors and experiences, and the spiritually uplifting way in which food is presented sends me home filled with inspirations.

There are many who regard chocolate as Nirvana, and certainly it's heavenly when combined with tropical fruits and either freshly whipped cream or ice cream. Rich and sensuous, Chocolate Nirvana derives intense orange accents from Grand Marnier, and lovely flavor contrasts from assorted tropical fruits. Perfumed with the scent of almonds, this dense, rich flourless cake is ideal for the gluten intolerant.

BITTERSWEET FLOURLESS CHOCOLATE CAKE

ONE 9-INCH CAKE

SERVES 10

1½ cups unsalted butter, room temperature, cut into ¼-inch cubes, plus 2 teaspoons, melted but not hot, for greasing mold

16 ounces marzipan

1½ cups granulated sugar

8 large eggs

2 tablespoons Grand Marnier liqueur

3 teaspoons Trablit coffee extract (see page 105)

1¼ cups cocoa powder, sifted

1. Preheat the oven to 300°F. Grease the bottom and sides of a 9-inch coffee cake ring mold. (If using a paper baking mold, it is not necessary to grease.)

2. Working in 30-second intervals, gently warm the marzipan in the microwave until it is soft and pliable. Be careful not to overheat it to the point of cooking the marzipan.

3. In the bowl of a stand mixer fitted with the paddle attachment, beat the marzipan on high speed for 2 minutes. Reduce the mixer speed to medium and add the cubed butter. Beat until smooth, about 2 minutes. Scrape down the sides of the bowl, and continue to mix for another 2 minutes. Reduce the mixer speed to low and add the sugar. Increase the mixer speed to medium and continue to beat until the mixture is pale yellow in color and thick and batterlike, about 3 minutes.

4. Add the eggs one at a time, mixing until well combined. When all of the eggs have been added, beat for an additional 3 minutes, scraping down the sides of the bowl as necessary. Mix together the Grand Marnier and coffee extract and add to the eggs; mix until combined. Reduce the mixer speed to low and add the sifted cocoa powder. The batter should be thick and smooth. Tiny marzipan clumps will dissolve in the oven during baking; break up large marzipan clumps with your fingers, or strain the batter through a medium-mesh sieve.

5. Pour the batter into the prepared pan. Place the pan on a baking sheet in the center of the oven. Bake until the cake is firm to the touch with a brownielike appearance, but is still semi soft inside, about 80 minutes.

6. Remove the cake from the oven and allow to cool for 2 hours or overnight. Once fully cooled, remove the cake from the pan (see page 12) or peel off the paper baking mold, if using. Wrap tightly in plastic. The cake can be stored in the refrigerator for up to 2 days.

CHOCOLATE ORANGE GANACHE

6 ounces (¾ cup) semi-sweet chocolate chips

1.5 ounces (¼ cup) 70% bittersweet chocolate, chopped

⅔ cup heavy cream

Grated zest of ½ orange

1. Place the chocolate chips and chopped chocolate in a medium, heatproof mixing bowl.

2. Bring the cream and zest to a boil in a small, heavy saucepan over medium-high heat. Strain the orange-infused hot cream through a fine-mesh sieve into the chocolate and let sit for 5 minutes. Using a rubber spatula, stir slowly and gently in a circular motion until the mixture is fully combined and homogenous.

3. Transfer the chocolate mixture to a food processor and process to blend (or, using an immersion blender, blend to emulsify). The ganache should be thick and shiny. Pour the ganache into a clean bowl and allow to cool slightly. The Chocolate Orange Ganache should be made when the cake is ready to be finished and served.

ASSEMBLY AND DECOR

Bittersweet Flourless Chocolate Cake, baked and cooled

1 recipe Chocolate Orange Ganache

Choice of fresh fruit, such as:

1 ripe medium banana, peeled and sliced

1 ripe medium mango, peeled, pitted, and sliced

1 ripe medium kiwi fruit, peeled and sliced

1 pint fresh strawberries, hulled and halved

1 pint fresh raspberries

1 tablespoon strained apricot jam, gently heated until liquid but not hot

Mango, Raspberry, or Chocolate Sauce (pages 169–170) (optional)

Freshly whipped cream or creamy gelato (optional)

1. Place the unwrapped cake on a serving platter or on a doily-covered 10-inch cake round.

2. In the bowl of a stand mixer fitted with the whisk attachment, whip the Chocolate Orange Ganache until it is light and fluffy, about 2 minutes. The ganache will change color from a dark to a lighter brown. Remove the bowl from the mixer. Using a rubber spatula, scrape the whipped ganache onto the top of the cake. Use a metal spatula to spread the ganache evenly around the top of the cake. Arrange desired cut fruit decoratively on the top of the cake to cover the Chocolate Orange Ganache. Drizzle with the strained apricot jam.

3. Place the decorated cake in the refrigerator for 1 to 2 hours to ensure that the fruit adheres to the ganache. Let the cake sit at room temperature for 2 hours before serving, as this cake is best when allowed to soften.

4. Cut the cake into slices and serve with sauce and a dollop of freshly whipped cream or creamy gelato, if desired.

Lemon Ricotta Cake

Inspired by traditional American layer cakes and one of a trio of fruit-forward ricotta tortes in this book, this creamy cake filled with blueberries and blackberries is a popular choice for weddings. You don't need to be a lemon lover to enjoy a slice of this light and luscious dessert!

Finished with a smooth lemon buttercream, this cake boasts a simple, elegant decor. The "wow factor" is determined by your choice of accents, such as flowers, ribbons, seashells, fresh fruits, and any other items that complement the theme of the event. For example, you can substitute raspberries and strawberries for the dark berries specified in the recipe.

To make the project manageable at home, assemble and freeze the individual cake tiers several days in advance. Prepare the buttercream and decorate the cakes the day before the event, to allow them to defrost overnight in the refrigerator. The only work required the day you serve the cake will be to stack and decorate the tiers.

RICOTTA POUND CAKES

MAKES 1 THREE-TIERED WEDDING-STYLE CAKE

SERVES 40 TO 50

2 tablespoons unsalted butter, melted but not hot

9 large eggs

3 cups granulated sugar

1½ cups grapeseed or vegetable oil

1½ cups whole or skim milk ricotta

2 teaspoons freshly squeezed lemon juice

1 teaspoon vanilla extract

4½ cups all-purpose flour

4½ teaspoons baking powder

1. Preheat the oven to 300°F. Grease the bottom and sides of one each 6-by-3-inch, 8-by-3-inch, and 10-by-3-inch round cake pans with removable bottoms with the melted butter and line the bottoms with parchment paper rounds.

2. In the bowl of a stand mixer fitted with the whisk attachment, beat together the eggs and sugar at medium-high speed until the mixture is very thick and falls in heavy ribbons, about 7 minutes.

3. In a separate bowl, whisk together the oil, ricotta, lemon juice, and vanilla. Gently add the ricotta mixture to the egg mixture and whip just until blended.

4. Sift together the flour and baking powder. Add the sifted ingredients to the batter, mixing just until incorporated, scraping down the sides of the mixing bowl as needed. Do not overmix. If necessary, finish folding in the sifted ingredients by hand, using a rubber spatula.

5. Distribute the batter into the prepared cake pans as follows: 4¾ cups into the largest pan, 3 cups into the second largest pan, and the remaining batter into the smallest pan.

6. Place all the cake pans on the same rack in the center of the oven and bake until golden brown, about 50 minutes for the smallest cake, 55 minutes for the second largest, and 60 minutes for the largest, until a knife inserted into the center comes out clean and the top springs back lightly when touched.

7. Remove the cakes from the oven and allow them to cool completely. Once cooled, remove the cakes from the pans (see page 12) and peel the parchment paper from the bottom of each cake. Wrap each cake tightly in plastic wrap until ready to use. The cakes can be stored for up to 1 day at room temperature or in the freezer for up to 1 week.

LEMON SIMPLE SYRUP

½ cup granulated sugar

1 cup freshly squeezed lemon juice, strained

1. Combine the sugar with ¼ cup water in a small, heavy saucepan over medium-high heat and bring to a boil, stirring occasionally. Remove from the heat, pour into a clean bowl, and allow to cool.

2. Once fully cooled, stir in the lemon juice until combined. The Lemon Simple Syrup will keep for up to 1 day in an airtight container in the refrigerator.

LEMON CURD

2 gelatin sheets (see page 11)

1¾ cups granulated sugar

1½ cups freshly squeezed lemon juice, strained

Grated zest of 2 lemons

7 large eggs

2 cups unsalted butter, room temperature, cut into ¼-inch cubes

1. Soften the gelatin sheets in 2 cups cool water for 5 minutes.

2. Combine the sugar, lemon juice, zest, and eggs in a heatproof, nonreactive mixing bowl over a saucepan of simmering water (do not allow the bowl to touch the water). Cook, whisking continuously, until the mixture boils and thickens, about 5 minutes. If using a candy thermometer, cook to 190°F.

3. Remove the bowl from over the water and whisk in the butter until fully combined. The curd should be smooth and homogenous.

4. Squeeze out the excess water from the softened gelatin and whisk the gelatin into the hot mixture until fully dissolved and combined. Strain the curd through a fine-mesh sieve into a clean, nonreactive mixing bowl. Cover with plastic wrap pressed directly onto the surface of the curd and allow to cool at room temperature for approximately 1 hour.

5. Divide the Lemon Curd into 2 portions: 3¼ cups to be used when assembling the cakes and ¼ cup to be used in the Lemon Buttercream recipe. Store all, covered, in the refrigerator at least 3 hours or overnight. The Lemon Curd can be made up to 3 days in advance.

2 pints fresh blackberries

2 pints fresh blueberries

1 (10-ounce) jar blackberry preserves

1 recipe Lemon Simple Syrup

3¼ cups Lemon Curd

6 cups heavy cream

⅔ cup granulated sugar

Ricotta Pound Cakes, baked and cooled

1. In a mixing bowl, combine the blackberries, blueberries, and ½ cup blackberry preserves. Set aside until ready to use.

2. Divide the Lemon Simple Syrup as follows: ¾ cup to be used on the 10-inch cake layer, ½ cup to used on the 8-inch cake layer, and ¼ cup to used on the 6-inch cake layer.

3. In a small bowl, whisk ¾ cup Lemon Curd to loosen and set aside.

4. In the bowl of a stand mixer fitted with the whisk attachment, whip together the cream and sugar until stiff peaks form, about 3 minutes. Remove the bowl from the mixer. Using a rubber spatula, fold in 2½ cups of the Lemon Curd until fully combined and the whipped cream has taken on a light yellow tint and bright, lemony flavor.

5. Working with 1 cake at a time, place the unwrapped cake on a flat work surface. Using a long serrated knife, slice off the top ⅛ to ¼ inch to even out the top of the cake as necessary. Slice the cake horizontally into 3 even layers.

6. Place a cardboard cake circle of corresponding size into each corresponding size cake pan in place of its removable bottom (see page 13). Place the bottom cake layer of each cake on top of its appropriate-sized cardboard circle, cut side up. Using a pastry brush, moisten each cake layer with one-third of its corresponding amount of Lemon Simple Syrup.

7. Using an offset spatula, spread the lemon curd whipped cream evenly onto each syrup-soaked cake layer as follows: 2 cups for the 10-inch layer, 1⅓ cups for the 8-inch layer, and ¾ cup for the 6-inch layer.

8. Using an offset spatula, spread a thin layer of the loosened Lemon Curd over the whipped cream as follows: ¼ cup for the 10-inch layer, and 2 tablespoons each for both the 8-inch layer and 6-inch layer.

9. Cover the Lemon Curd layer with the berry mixture as follows: 1 cup for the 10-inch layer, ½ cup for the 8-inch layer, and ⅓ cup for the 6-inch layer.

10. Top each with a second layer of cake and repeat with another one-third of its corresponding amount of Lemon Simple Syrup, whipped cream as above, Lemon Curd as above, and berries. Don't worry if there is slightly less lemon curd whipped cream for this second and final layer.

11. Top each with its final layer of cake and moisten with the remaining syrup. Tightly wrap each cake in the pan in plastic wrap and place in the freezer overnight or for up to 1 week. If you are freezing the cakes for longer than 24 hours, make sure to double- or triple-wrap each cake to protect from freezer odors.

½ cup whole milk

½ teaspoon vanilla extract

¾ cup granulated sugar

8 large egg yolks

3⅓ cups unsalted butter,
room temperature,
cut into ¼-inch cubes

1 recipe Italian Meringue
(see page 22)

¼ cup Lemon Curd

¼ cup freshly squeezed
lemon juice, strained

1. In a medium, heavy saucepan over medium-high heat, bring the milk, vanilla, and 6 tablespoons sugar to a boil.

2. Meanwhile, whisk together the remaining sugar and the egg yolks in a heatproof, nonreactive mixing bowl until well combined and smooth. While whisking continuously, slowly pour the warm milk mixture into the egg mixture and whisk until well incorporated. Return the milk-egg mixture to the saucepan, insert a candy thermometer, and cook over medium heat, stirring gently with a rubber spatula until the mixture begins to thicken and has reached 150°F, 3 to 4 minutes. Strain the mixture through a fine-mesh sieve into the clean bowl of a stand mixer fitted with a whisk attachment. Whip on medium-high speed until cooled, thickened, and pale yellow in color, about 10 minutes.

3. Reduce the mixer speed to low and add the butter ½ cup at a time until fully incorporated. Add the Italian Meringue, increasing the mixer speed as necessary to fully incorporate. Once fully combined, remove the bowl from the mixer. Using a hand whisk, whisk in the Lemon Curd, followed by the lemon juice, until smooth.

4. I recommend making the buttercream when you are ready to frost and finish the cakes for optimal texture and creaminess. Cover all with plastic wrap and if you are not using immediately, refrigerate until ready to use, but for no longer than 24 hours because the lemon flavor can change. If refrigerated, allow the Lemon Buttercream to come to room temperature before using or gently reheat the buttercream in the microwave in eight 10- to 20-second intervals, whisking vigorously by hand after each interval, to obtain the buttercream's original texture.

DECOR

1 recipe Lemon Buttercream

1 fresh cardboard round
for each layer (10-inch, 8-inch,
and 6-inch)

3 (12-inch, ¼-inch-diameter)
wooden dowels

3 square cardboard boxes
(10-by-5-inch, 8-by-5-inch,
and 6-by-5-inch)

1. Working with 1 cake tier at a time, remove each assembled cake from the freezer and remove the plastic wrap. Using a long metal spatula, evenly top each cake in its pan with a smooth and flat layer of freshly made or softened Lemon Buttercream as follows: about ¼ cup for the 6-inch cake, ⅓-cup for the 8-inch cake, and ½ to ¾ cup for the 10-inch cake. Return the cakes to the freezer, unwrapped, for approximately 1 hour to allow the buttercream to set.

2. Working with 1 cake tier at a time, remove each cake from the freezer and unmold it from its cake pan (see page 14). Transfer each cake onto a clean cardboard cake round. Using an offset spatula, spread a thin layer of Lemon Buttercream over the side of each cake, as smoothly and evenly as possible. Return each cake to the freezer to firm up while you repeat with the remaining cakes. Repeat until all 3 cakes are covered in a buttercream layer. It may take up to 60 minutes for the buttercream layer to firm up completely in the freezer before applying a second layer.

3. Apply a second, slightly thicker coat of Lemon Buttercream to each cake, making sure to apply this as evenly as possible. Once all the buttercream has been applied, smooth it out by dipping the blade of the offset spatula in hot water, shaking off the excess water, and running the blade of the spatula over any rough spots, patching with leftover buttercream as needed to create a very even texture.

4. It is important to cut the dowels so that they are the same height as the cake tier into which they are being inserted. The most exact way to measure is by inserting the dowel into its corresponding cake tier. Mark the dowel where it comes out of the cake and then use a very sharp serrated knife, or wire cutters, to cut it to size. You will need 4 dowels for each of the two larger cakes. The smallest cake will not need dowels as it is the top tier of the stacked cake.

5. For the 8-inch cake tier: Imagine a 3-inch-diameter circle in the center of the cake. Evenly space 4 dowels around that circle and press them firmly into the cake until they hit the cardboard cake round at the bottom. If the dowels have been measured and cut properly, they will not stick up out of the top of the cake. Repeat the same procedure with the 10-inch cake tier, using an imaginary 4-inch-diameter circle as your guide for where to place the dowels.

6. Place each cake tier in its own properly sized cardboard cake box in the refrigerator overnight to defrost. By storing the cakes in boxes, they will be protected from odors in the refrigerator and possibly being bumped. Defrost the cake tiers in the refrigerator for 12 hours before attempting to stack.

TO STACK AND FINISH

Flowers, ribbons, cake stand, and other accents as desired

3 yards of ribbon (if using ribbon)

3 pearlhead pins (if using ribbon)

Blackberry Sauce (page 168) (optional)

1. Remove the largest cake tier from its box and cut ribbon to fit around its base. Use a pearlhead pin to secure and repeat with the other 2 tiers. Store all of the tiers in refrigerator until ready to display.

2. Remove the largest cake tier from its box and, using an offset spatula, place on your choice of a cake stand or platter. Remove the middle cake tier from its box and carefully center it over the dowels, placing it gently onto the bottom tier. Repeat the procedure with the last cake.

3. Style with your flowers or choice of accents. Place and display for guests. The cake can be displayed at room temperature for up to 3 hours before slicing and serving.

4. When you are ready to serve, take apart the tiered cakes and begin slicing the 10-inch cake with a sharp knife. After each slice, rinse the knife in hot water, so that the appearance of each piece is very clean. You should get 20 slices out of the 10-inch cake. Slice the 8-inch cake the same way; you should get 15 slices out of the 8-inch cake. You should get 8 to 10 slices from the 6-inch cake. Serve slices with sauce, if desired.

Strawberry Shortcakes

Every summer, San Diego farmers grow the most delicious organic strawberries, and I love making desserts that take advantage of this abundance. My strawberry shortcake updates the classic American recipe by replacing the whipped cream filling with white chocolate mousse.

Because the shortcake itself is dense and sconelike, I prefer to serve it with a pool of fresh strawberry sauce to heighten both presentation and flavor. For optimum texture and taste appeal, I suggest making the shortcakes the day they are to be served.

Choose uniformly shaped, medium-size strawberries that yield 5 thin slices each. Smaller slices lack visual impact, and too-large slices are difficult to arrange.

BUTTERMILK SHORTCAKES

MAKES 10 THREE-INCH ROUND OR
FLOWER-SHAPED SHORTCAKES

SERVES 10

¾ cup unsalted butter, room
temperature, plus 2 teaspoons,
melted but not hot, for sheets

1¼ cups granulated sugar

2 large egg yolks

1 teaspoon vanilla extract

5¾ cups all-purpose flour

1½ teaspoons baking soda

3 teaspoons baking powder

½ teaspoon ground cinnamon

½ teaspoon ground cardamom

1 teaspoon ground allspice

1 teaspoon salt

1⅓ cups buttermilk

2 tablespoons heavy cream

¼ cup sliced almonds

1. Preheat the oven to 300°F. Lightly grease 1 large or 2 smaller baking sheets with the 2 teaspoons melted butter or line with a Silpat.

2. In the bowl of a stand mixer fitted with the paddle attachment, beat together the butter and sugar until softened and less sandy in texture, about 3 minutes. Using a rubber spatula, scrape down the sides of the bowl as needed and slowly add the egg yolks and vanilla. Continue mixing for another 2 minutes.

3. Reduce the mixer speed to low. With the machine running, sift all the dry ingredients together into the bowl little by little, mixing just until incorporated, being very careful not to overmix. Add the buttermilk and mix just until blended. The dough should be very moist.

4. Scrape the dough out onto a lightly floured sheet of parchment paper or a Silpat. Pat the dough into a rectangular shape about 1 inch thick. Cover with plastic wrap and use a rolling pin to roll out to ¾ inch thick.

5. Dip a 3-inch cutter in flour, then press it into the dough to cut out individual shortcakes. You may need to pat the dough scraps together and gently roll out again in order to get 10 shortcakes. Place on the prepared baking sheet, allowing enough room in between each for spreading. Brush the top with cream and sprinkle with almond slices. Bake until colored slightly but still moist to the touch, about 45 minutes. Let cool completely.

WHITE CHOCOLATE SOUR CREAM MOUSSE

¾ cup sour cream, room
temperature

7 ounces (generous 1 cup)
good-quality white chocolate,
coarsely chopped

½ cup heavy cream

1. Place the sour cream in a bowl and whisk quickly to loosen. If it is colder than room temperature, warm it in a microwave.

2. Place the chocolate in a medium, heatproof mixing bowl.

3. Bring the heavy cream to a boil in a small, heavy saucepan over medium-high heat. Pour the hot cream over the white chocolate and let sit for a couple of minutes before whisking until smooth and fully combined.

4. Using a whisk, mix the sour cream into the white chocolate ganache in 2 additions. Cover with plastic wrap pressed directly onto the surface of the mousse and refrigerate overnight to set. The mousse can be made up to 2 days in advance and stored in the refrigerator, tightly covered; it can be used directly from the refrigerator.

ASSEMBLY

4 cups heavy cream

¼ cup plus 2 tablespoons
granulated sugar

20 equal-sized fresh medium
strawberries, hulled, sliced
into 4 or 5 slices each

Buttermilk Shortcakes,
baked and cooled

⅓ cup strained raspberry
preserves

1 recipe White Chocolate
Sour Cream Mousse

1. Whip together the cream and sugar in the bowl of a stand mixer fitted with the whisk attachment until stiff peaks form, about 3 minutes. Measure out ½ cup of whipped cream and set aside to be used in the final decor. Fit a pastry bag with a ¼-inch, 8-point closed star decorating tip and fill with the remaining whipped cream. Hold all in the refrigerator.

2. Cut each shortcake in half horizontally and place each half on a flat work surface, cut side up. Brush the cut side of each shortcake with the preserves.

3. Fit a pastry bag with a ¼-inch plain round decorating tip and fill with the mousse. Pipe the mousse onto the bottom half of each shortcake, stopping ½ inch from the edge of the shortcake.

4. Layer overlapping strawberry slices around the border. Pipe ⅓ cup whipped cream over the mousse-and-strawberry layer and cover with the top of the shortcake. Refrigerate the assembled shortcakes for 3 hours before serving, to give them a chance to settle.

DECOR

¼ cup powdered sugar

Reserved ½ cup whipped cream

3 equal-sized medium
strawberries, hulled, quartered
lengthwise

10 spray roses or 20 rose petals

Strawberry Sauce and Raspberry
Sauce (page 170)

1. Remove the assembled shortcakes from the refrigerator. Using a small sieve, generously sprinkle the shortcakes with the powdered sugar.

2. Fill a pastry bag fitted with a ¼-inch, 8-point closed star decorating tip with the whipped cream and pipe one small rosette on top of each shortcake. Top each rosette with a strawberry piece and garnish with flower petals or an individual spray rose.

3. Arrange the Strawberry Shortcakes on a serving platter and keep refrigerated until ready to serve. The shortcakes can be displayed at room temperature for up to 1 hour. Serve with sauce.

Caribe

The delicious flavor of passion fruit harmonizes beautifully with many other elements. Naturally sweet, yet slightly tangy with a hint of citrus, passion fruit blends well with robust dark chocolate. I first experienced this superb pairing on a culinary trip to Paris to study under renowned pastry chef Christophe Felder at Bellouet Conseil. Caribe is my tribute to this stunning combination of tropical flavors.

While passion fruit puree (see page 11) is preferable for this recipe, passion fruit juice may be substituted. However, it will result in a somewhat sweeter, less intense flavor. Note that the assembly requires an 8-inch dome-shaped mold.

DARK CHOCOLATE CAKE

MAKES ONE 8-INCH DOME CAKE

SERVES 12 TO 14

2 tablespoons unsalted butter, plus 2 teaspoons, melted but not hot, for greasing pan

1 ounce (⅛ cup) unsweetened chocolate, finely chopped

⅓ cup plus 1 tablespoon all-purpose flour

¼ cup cocoa powder

1 large egg

6 large egg yolks

¼ cup plus 3 tablespoons granulated sugar

1 tablespoon honey

4 large egg whites

1. Preheat the oven to 300°F. Grease the bottom and sides of an 8-by-3-inch round cake pan with removable bottom with the 2 teaspoons melted butter and line the bottom with an 8-inch-diameter parchment paper round.

2. Combine the chocolate and 2 tablespoons butter in a microwave-safe mixing bowl and heat in the microwave until melted and smooth, or melt together in small, heavy saucepan over very low heat, stirring continuously. The chocolate mixture should be warm but not hot.

3. Sift together the flour and cocoa powder and set aside.

4. Combine the whole egg, egg yolks, ¼ cup sugar, and honey in the bowl of a stand mixer fitted with the whisk attachment. Whip on medium-high speed until light in color and thick in volume, about 7 minutes. Add the melted chocolate and butter, whipping until fully combined. Remove the bowl from the mixer. Using a rubber spatula, gently fold in the sifted ingredients until combined. Transfer to a clean bowl large enough to mix in the meringue (see step 7).

5. In the bowl of a stand mixer fitted with the whisk attachment, whip the egg whites on medium speed for 2 minutes. When the egg whites are frothy, begin to slowly add the remaining 3 tablespoons sugar and increase the mixer speed to medium-high. Whip until the egg whites are stiff with a creamy texture, about 3 minutes. Remove the bowl from the mixer.

6. Using a rubber spatula, carefully fold the meringue into the batter in 3 additions.

7. Pour the batter into the prepared cake pan and place on a rack in the center of the oven. Bake until the cake is firm to the touch yet still appears moist, about 30 minutes.

8. Remove the cake from the oven and allow to cool completely. Once cooled, remove the cake from the pan (see page 12) and peel the parchment paper from the bottom of the cake. Wrap the cake tightly in plastic wrap until ready to use. The Dark Chocolate Cake can be stored for up to 1 day at room temperature.

PASSION FRUIT SIMPLE SYRUP

¼ cup granulated sugar

½ cup passion fruit puree

1. Combine the sugar with 2 tablespoons water in a small, heavy saucepan over medium-high heat and bring to a boil, stirring occasionally. Remove from the heat, pour into a clean bowl, and allow to cool.

2. Once fully cooled, stir in the passion fruit puree until combined. The Passion Fruit Simple Syrup will keep for up to 2 days in an airtight container in the refrigerator.

SEMISWEET CHOCOLATE GANACHE

18 ounces (3 cups) semisweet chocolate chips

1½ cups heavy cream

2 teaspoons Myer's dark rum

1. Place the chocolate chips in a medium, heatproof mixing bowl.

2. Bring the cream to a boil in a small, heavy saucepan over medium-high heat. Pour the hot cream over the chocolate and let sit for 5 minutes. Using a rubber spatula, stir slowly and gently in a circular motion until mixture is fully combined and homogenous.

3. Transfer the chocolate mixture to a food processor; add the rum and process to blend (or, using an immersion blender, add the rum to the bowl with the chocolate and cream and blend to emulsify). The ganache should be thick and shiny.

4. Pour the ganache into a clean bowl and allow to cool and firm to the consistency of pudding. The Semisweet Chocolate Ganache can be made up to 5 days in advance and kept in an airtight container in the refrigerator, but may need to be gently reheated before using (see page 12).

CHOCOLATE PASSION FRUIT MOUSSE

2½ cups heavy cream

7 ounces (1⅓ cup) 64% bittersweet chocolate, chopped

4 ounces (⅔ cup) 33% to 40% milk chocolate, chopped

⅓ cup granulated sugar

4 large egg yolks

½ cup (1 small to medium) sliced ripe banana

⅓ cup passion fruit puree

2 tablespoons unsalted butter, room temperature, cut into ¼-inch cubes

1. In the bowl of a stand mixer fitted with the whisk attachment, whip 2 cups heavy cream until soft peaks form, 2 to 3 minutes. Hold in the refrigerator until ready to use.

2. Melt together both chocolates in a large, heatproof mixing bowl set over a saucepan of simmering water (do not allow the bowl to touch the water), stirring occasionally. The melted chocolate should be warm but not hot. Remove the bowl from over the water and set aside.

3. Combine the sugar with ¼ cup water in a small, heavy saucepan over medium-high heat and bring to a boil. Insert a candy thermometer and cook to 230° to 240°F, the soft-ball stage.

4. While the sugar is cooking, place the egg yolks in the bowl of a stand mixer fitted with the whisk attachment and whip at medium-high speed until thick and light, about 3 minutes. Carefully pour the hot sugar syrup into the whipping yolks in a continuous stream, being careful to avoid pouring the syrup directly onto the moving whisk. Increase the mixer speed to high and whisk until mixture has cooled down and has tripled in volume, 7 to 10 minutes.

5. While the yolk mixture is cooling, blend together the banana and passion fruit puree in the bowl of a food processor fitted with the blade attachment until liquid. Pour into a clean mixing bowl.

6. Combine the remaining ½ cup heavy cream with the butter in a small, heavy saucepan over medium heat and bring to a boil, stirring occasionally. Pour about one-third of the hot cream mixture into the pureed fruit and immediately whisk to combine. Whisk in the remaining hot cream until well incorporated. Slowly strain the hot mixture through a fine-mesh sieve into the melted chocolate in several additions, whisking continuously. Stir vigorously until fully combined, smooth, and homogenous. The chocolate should look shiny and glossy.

7. Remove the cooled egg mixture from the mixer. Using a rubber spatula, fold the egg mixture into the chocolate in several additions until fully combined. Then fold in the whipped cream until well blended. The Chocolate Passion Fruit Mousse should be made when ready to assemble the cake.

ASSEMBLY

Dark Chocolate Cake, baked and cooled

1 recipe Semisweet Chocolate Ganache

5 cups Chocolate Passion Fruit Mousse

1 recipe Passion Fruit Simple Syrup

1. Place the unwrapped cake on a flat work surface. Using a long serrated knife, slice the cake horizontally into 2 even layers. Trim one layer down to a 4-inch-diameter circle.

2. Measure out 1¾ cups Semisweet Chocolate Ganache and set aside to be used in the Decor portion. Gently warm the remaining ganache (see page 12) until soft enough to spread easily.

3. Pour 1 cup of Semisweet Chocolate Ganache into the dome mold and use a pastry brush, the back of a spoon, or clean hands to spread the ganache evenly around the inside of the mold until completely coated with chocolate. Place the mold in the freezer to allow the ganache to set, about 30 minutes. When firm, coat with another ½ cup of ganache to create a solid ganache shell. Return the mold to the freezer to firm, about 30 minutes. When the ganache is firm, remove the mold from the freezer and place 2½ cups Chocolate Passion Fruit Mousse into the center of the mold.

4. Using a pastry brush, lightly moisten the cut side of the trimmed 4-inch cake layer with approximately 2 tablespoons Passion Fruit Simple Syrup.

5. Using an offset spatula, spread approximately ¼ cup of warmed ganache onto the moistened cake layer. Place this ganache-covered cake layer over the mousse layer in the dome mold, ganache side down, and press gently. Top with the remaining 2½ cups Chocolate Passion Fruit Mousse.

6. Moisten the cut side of the remaining 8-inch cake layer with the remaining Passion Fruit Simple Syrup and spread with the remaining Semisweet Chocolate Ganache. Place the cake layer ganache side down over the mousse and press down firmly. It should now be even with the top edge of the dome mold. Tightly wrap the cake in the pan in plastic wrap and place in the freezer overnight.

Reserved 1¾ cups Semisweet
Chocolate Ganache

¼ cup cocoa powder

2 ripe medium bananas,
cut into 40 (¼-inch) slices

1 teaspoon freshly squeezed
lemon juice

Chocolate and Mango
or Passion Fruit Sauce
(page 169) (optional)

1. Remove the assembled cake from the freezer, remove the plastic wrap, and unmold the cake from the mold (see page 14). Transfer the frozen cake to an 8-inch round cake board and place the cake with the cake board on a wire cooling rack set over a baking sheet.

2. Fit a pastry bag with a ¼-inch round decorating tip and fill with 2 tablespoons of Semisweet Chocolate Ganache; hold at room temperature until ready to use. Gently warm the remaining ganache until liquid and thick (see page 12). Pour the warmed, liquid ganache directly over the top of cake to completely cover. Place in the refrigerator for 6 to 8 hours to allow the ganache to firm and the cake to fully defrost.

3. One hour before serving, remove the cake from the refrigerator. Using a fine-mesh sieve, dust the surface of the cake generously with cocoa powder to completely cover. Place the cake on a serving plate.

4. Brush the banana slices lightly with lemon juice. Using the Semisweet Chocolate Ganache-filled pastry bag, dot each banana slice with ganache and adhere the slices to the bottom edge of the cake, over-lapping the slices to create a border.

5. Allow the decorated cake to sit at room temperature for 1 hour before serving. Serve slices with sauce, if desired.

Bora Bora

The flavors and textures of this coconut cream torte remind me of many happy visits to the South Pacific. Eating freshly picked coconut while trekking around the islands is a particularly vivid memory, since the juice was so clean and sweet, and the meat unexpectedly soft and tender. For someone who loves coconut, Bora Bora is pure heaven.

This recipe uses three kinds of coconut: fine-cut, sometimes referred to as macaroon coconut; medium-shred, which is similar to the type used in German Chocolate Cake; and large chip or flake coconut, which primarily is used for decor. Because of the varying textures, each has specific uses and should not be substituted for the others.

Although something of a challenge to find, frozen coconut milk puree (see page 171) is preferable to coconut milk due to its creamy qualities and true coconut taste. In a bind, use canned coconut milk but expect a less intense flavor. If you do not use frozen coconut milk puree, omit the glaze and frost the cake with whipped cream, finishing the top and sides with large flake coconut and powdered sugar (see Vallarta on page 164). An alternative finish would be to press coconut cookies around the sides and pipe whipped cream rosettes on top (see Strawberry Poppy Seed Cake on page 98).

VANILLA JOCONDE

MAKES ONE 10-INCH CAKE

SERVES 16 TO 18

2 teaspoons unsalted
butter, melted but not hot

2 large eggs

5 large egg yolks

½ cup granulated sugar

1 cup all-purpose flour

1 cup plus 2 tablespoons
powdered sugar, sifted

1½ cups almond flour

8 large egg whites

1. Preheat the oven to 325°F. Grease the bottom and sides of a 10-by-3-inch round cake pan with removable bottom with the melted butter, and line the bottom with a 10-inch-diameter parchment paper round.

2. In the bowl of a stand mixer fitted with the whisk attachment, whip together the whole eggs and egg yolks with ¼ cup granulated sugar on medium-high speed for 3 minutes. Increase the mixer speed to high and whip until light in color and thick, about 3 minutes more.

3. While the eggs are whipping, sift together the all-purpose flour and powdered sugar. Place these, together with the almond flour, in the bowl of a food processor fitted with the blade attachment and process until the mixture is finely ground.

4. Reduce the mixer speed to low and add the freshly processed mixture to the eggs, blending only just until combined, being careful not to overmix the batter. Transfer the batter to a clean mixing bowl large enough to mix in the meringue (see step 6).

5. In the bowl of a stand mixer fitted with the whisk attachment, whip the egg whites on medium speed for 2 minutes. When the egg whites are frothy, begin to slowly add the remaining ¼ cup granulated sugar and increase the mixer speed to medium-high. Whip until the egg whites are stiff with a creamy texture, about 3 minutes. Remove the bowl from the mixer.

6. Using a rubber spatula, carefully fold the meringue into the batter in 3 additions.

7. Pour the batter into the prepared cake pan and place on a rack in the center of the oven. Bake the cake until a knife inserted in the center comes out clean, about 40 minutes. The cake will have a slightly golden color and a spongelike texture.

8. Remove the cake from the oven and allow to cool completely. Once cooled, remove the cake from the pan (see page 12) and peel the parchment paper from the bottom of the cake. Wrap the cake tightly in plastic wrap until ready to use. The Vanilla Joconde can be stored for up to 1 day in the refrigerator or in the freezer for up to 1 week.

COCONUT MILK SIMPLE SYRUP

¼ cup granulated sugar

½ cup frozen coconut milk puree, thawed

1. Combine the sugar with ¼ cup water in a small, heavy saucepan over medium-high heat and bring to a boil, stirring occasionally. Remove from the heat, pour into a clean bowl, and allow to cool.

2. Once fully cooled, stir in the coconut milk puree until combined. The Coconut Milk Simple Syrup will keep for up to 2 days in an airtight container in the refrigerator.

COCONUT CREAM

1⅓ cups whole milk

2 teaspoons vanilla extract

1 cup unsweetened medium shredded coconut

⅓ cup granulated sugar

1 tablespoon plus
2 teaspoons all-purpose flour

2 large eggs

¼ cup unsalted butter,
room temperature,
cut into ¼-inch cubes

1. Place the first 6 ingredients in a heatproof mixing bowl set over a pan of simmering water (do not allow the bowl to touch the water). Whisk continuously until the mixture cooks and thickens to a custardlike consistency, about 5 minutes. If using a candy thermometer, cook to 185°F. Remove the mixing bowl from over the water and whisk in the butter until smooth and homogenous.

2. Pour into a clean bowl, cover with plastic wrap pressed directly onto the surface of the cream, and cool in the refrigerator for 1 hour. The Coconut Cream can be made up to 3 days in advance.

¾ cup frozen coconut milk
puree, thawed

1¼ cups heavy cream

1 teaspoon vanilla extract

¼ cup granulated sugar

3 extra-large egg yolks

2 tablespoons cornstarch

1 tablespoon unsalted
butter, room temperature,
cut into ¼-inch cubes

1 gelatin sheet (see page 11)

1. Combine ½ cup coconut milk puree, ¼ cup heavy cream, and the vanilla in a medium, heavy saucepan over medium-high heat and bring to a boil.

2. Whisk together the sugar, egg yolks, and cornstarch in a heatproof, nonreactive mixing bowl until well combined and smooth. While whisking continuously, slowly pour the hot cream mixture into the egg mixture and whisk until well incorporated. Strain through a medium-mesh sieve back into the saucepan and continue to cook over medium heat, whisking continuously, until the mixture begins to boil and has thickened to a custard, about 5 minutes. If using a candy thermometer, cook to 160°F. Strain the mixture through a fine-mesh sieve into a clean, nonreactive mixing bowl and whisk in the butter until smooth and fully combined.

3. Soften the gelatin sheet in 2 cups cool water for 5 minutes. Squeeze out the excess water, then melt the gelatin in a small saucepan over low heat until liquid. Whisk the liquid gelatin into the warm custard until fully dissolved and the custard is smooth. Cover with plastic wrap pressed directly onto the surface of the custard and cool in the refrigerator for 1 hour.

4. Once the custard has cooled and is ready to use, remove it from the refrigerator.

5. In the bowl of a stand mixer fitted with the whisk attachment, whip the remaining 1 cup heavy cream until soft peaks form, about 1 minute. Hold in the refrigerator until ready to use.

6. In the bowl of a stand mixer fitted with either the whisk or the paddle attachment, gently beat the cooled custard to loosen. Add the remaining ¼ cup coconut milk puree and mix just until combined. Remove the bowl from the mixer. Using a rubber spatula, gently fold in the whipped cream until just combined. The Coconut Cream Mousse should be made the same day you assemble the cake or it will become too stiff to use.

ASSEMBLY

2 cups heavy cream

2 tablespoons granulated sugar

Vanilla Joconde, baked and cooled

1 recipe Coconut Milk Simple Syrup

1 recipe Coconut Cream Mousse

1 recipe Coconut Cream

1. In the bowl of a stand mixer fitted with the whisk attachment, whip together the heavy cream and sugar until stiff peaks form, about 2 minutes. Fit a pastry bag with a ½-inch plain round decorating tip and fill with half of the whipped cream. Hold all in the refrigerator until ready to use.

2. Place the unwrapped joconde on a flat work surface. Using a long serrated knife, slice off the top ¼ inch to even out the top of the cake as necessary. Slice the cake horizontally into three ¼-inch-thick layers.

3. Using a 10-inch round cake board as the bottom of a 10-by-3-inch round cake pan with removable bottom (see page 13), place 1 cake layer on the cake board, cut side up. Using a pastry brush, moisten the cake layer with one-third of the Coconut Milk Simple Syrup.

4. Using an offset spatula, spread 1¼ cups of the Coconut Cream Mousse evenly over the syrup-soaked cake layer, all the way to the edges of the cake and side of the pan. Cover with approximately ⅔ cup of the Coconut Cream. Using the filled pastry bag, pipe a layer of whipped cream over the Coconut Cream, using up the entire bag. Refill the bag with the remaining whipped cream to be used on the next layer.

5. Top with the second layer of joconde and repeat with another one-third of the syrup, the remaining Coconut Cream Mousse, another ⅔ cup of the Coconut Cream, and the remaining whipped cream.

6. Top with the final layer of cake and moisten with the remaining Coconut Milk Simple Syrup. Cover with the remaining Coconut Cream. Tightly wrap the cake in the pan in plastic wrap and place in the freezer overnight.

COCONUT CREAM GLAZE

2 gelatin sheets (see page 11)

⅓ cup plus 2 tablespoons frozen coconut milk puree, thawed

⅓ cup glucose or light corn syrup

1. Soften the gelatin sheets in 2 cups cool water for 5 minutes.

2. In a medium, heavy saucepan over medium-high heat, bring the coconut milk puree and glucose to a boil. Remove from the heat.

3. Squeeze out the excess water from the gelatin, then melt the gelatin in a small saucepan over low heat until liquid. Stir the melted gelatin into the hot coconut mixture and whisk until blended and smooth. Allow the Coconut Cream Glaze to cool at room temperature for 15 minutes before using. The glaze should be made when ready to decorate the cake.

COCONUT COOKIES

1½ cups unsweetened
macaroon or fine-cut coconut

⅔ cup granulated sugar

1 tablespoon plus 2 teaspoons
all-purpose flour

2 large eggs

1. Preheat the oven to 300°F.

2. Combine all the ingredients in the bowl of a stand mixer fitted with the paddle attachment and mix to form a dough. (You can also work the ingredients together by hand, using a wooden spoon.) Remove the bowl from the mixer. Place the dough on a large sheet of parchment paper or on a Silpat.

3. Pat the dough into a rectangle about ½ inch thick. Cover with a piece of plastic wrap and use a rolling pin to roll out the dough as evenly as possible to a very thin rectangle, approximately ¼ inch thick. Peel away the plastic wrap and transfer the dough to a baking sheet, keeping the parchment paper or Silpat under the dough.

4. Transfer the baking sheet to a rack in the center of the oven and bake until the dough is slightly browned, about 20 minutes.

5. Remove the dough from the oven and allow to cool slightly. While still warm, use a paring knife to score the dough into 3-by-1¼-inch cookies. You will need a minimum of 25 cookies to decorate the outside of the cake. Allow the dough to finish cooling and cut the scored cookies out completely. The Coconut Cookies can be made 1 day in advance and stored in an airtight container at room temperature.

DECOR

1 recipe Coconut Cream Glaze

1 recipe Coconut Cookies

Vanilla Sauce and Mango
Sauce or Tropical Fruit Sauce
(pages 169–170) (optional)

1. Remove the assembled cake from the freezer and remove the plastic wrap. Pour enough warm Coconut Cream Glaze onto the top of the frozen cake to generously coat, swirling the cake pan around to evenly distribute the glaze. Return the cake to the freezer to allow the glaze to harden for 30 minutes.

2. Once the glaze has set, remove the cake from the freezer and unmold the cake from the pan (see page 14). Place the unmolded cake in the refrigerator to defrost overnight, or for a minimum of 10 hours.

3. Remove the defrosted cake from the refrigerator up to 1 hour before serving. Place the cake on a serving platter and press the Coconut Cookies vertically around the outside of the cake. Serve slices with sauce, if desired.

Citronesse

I created this lemon cheesecake early in my career, while working at one of Cancun's finest restaurants. Taking advantage of the bounty of fresh tropical fruit, I used local lemons that tasted somewhat of lime and were *very* tart. Over the years, this cake has undergone many tweaks and reincarnations, and remains a favorite among lemon lovers. The lemon flavor resonates throughout the cake, both in a filling enriched with lemon curd and in a separate lemon curd layer. An ode to classic lemon meringue pie, the meringue imparts a sweet, caramelized flavor.

This cheesecake is best made and baked 1 day in advance, but for maximum freshness, make the meringue the day it will be served. And note that although the meringue supplies a delicious and stunning decor, it can be omitted, since this cake is so wonderful on its own.

Before getting started, be sure that all the ingredients are at room temperature to avoid lumps in the batter and in the finished cake.

PECAN GRAHAM CRACKER CRUST

MAKES ONE 10-INCH CAKE

SERVES 14 TO 16

⅓ cup unsalted butter,
melted but not hot,
plus 2 teaspoons,
for greasing pan

1 cup or 1 sleeve
graham crackers

½ cup pecans,
toasted and cooled

½ cup (tightly packed)
brown sugar

1. Preheat the oven to 250°F. Grease the bottom and sides of a 10-by-3-inch round cake pan with removable bottom or a 10-by-3-inch round springform pan with 2 teaspoons of the melted butter.

2. In the bowl of a food processor fitted with the blade attachment, pulse together the graham crackers and pecans to a fine powder. Transfer the mixture to a large mixing bowl and add the brown sugar. Using a rubber spatula, stir in the remaining ⅓ cup melted butter. Finish mixing by hand to ensure that the butter is well incorporated and the crust is evenly moist throughout.

3. Spread the mixture onto the bottom of the prepared pan and using a curved spatula or a fork, flatten the crust and pack it tightly into the bottom of the pan.

4. Bake the crust on a rack in the center of the oven until lightly toasted in appearance, about 45 minutes.

5. Remove the crust from the oven and allow to cool completely. Once fully cooled, wrap the Pecan Graham Cracker Crust in the pan tightly in plastic wrap until ready to use. The baked Pecan Graham Cracker Crust can be stored for up to 2 days in a dry, cool oven.

LEMON CURD

½ cup freshly squeezed
lemon juice, strained

1 cup granulated sugar

Grated zest of 1 lemon

4 large eggs

½ cup unsalted butter,
room temperature,
cut into ¼-inch cubes

1. Combine the first 4 ingredients in a heatproof, nonreactive mixing bowl over a pan of simmering water (do not allow the bowl to touch the water). Cook, whisking continuously, until the mixture is frothy and begins to thicken to a custard, about 4 minutes. If using a candy thermometer, cook to 190°F.

2. Remove the bowl from over the water and whisk in the butter until fully combined. The curd should be smooth and homogenous. Strain through a fine-mesh sieve into a clean, nonreactive mixing bowl. Measure out 1¼ cups of Lemon Curd to be used in the cheesecake filling; the remainder will be used to assemble the cake. Cover all with plastic wrap pressed directly onto the surface of the curd and cool in the refrigerator until ready to use. The Lemon Curd can be made up to 3 days in advance and stored in the refrigerator.

LEMON CHEESECAKE

5 (8-ounce) packages cream
cheese, room temperature

2 cups plus 3 tablespoons
granulated sugar

5 large eggs

2 teaspoons vanilla extract

1 cup sour cream,
room temperature

Pecan Graham Cracker
Crust, baked and cooled

1¼ cups Lemon Curd,
cooled

1. Preheat the oven to 300°F.

2. In the bowl of a stand mixer fitted with the paddle attachment, beat the cream cheese and sugar on medium-high speed until light and fluffy, about 6 minutes. Scrape down the sides of the bowl, reduce the mixer speed to low, and add the eggs one at a time, incorporating fully after each addition. Scrape down the sides of the bowl again as needed and add the vanilla and sour cream. Mix until fully combined and the batter is smooth. Pour the batter over the baked and cooled crust. Using a spoon or the back of a knife, swirl in the Lemon Curd to create a marbled effect.

3. Place the cake on a rack in the center of the oven and bake for about 1 hour and 50 minutes. The top may crack and the cake may turn a slight golden brown color. Remove the cheesecake from the oven and allow to cool completely before covering with plastic wrap and freezing overnight to set.

ASSEMBLY

1²⁄₃ cups Lemon Curd

Lemon Cheesecake, baked
and frozen overnight

1. Place the Lemon Curd in a heatproof, nonreactive mixing bowl set over a pan of simmering water (do not allow the bowl to touch the water) and whisk to soften. The desired consistency should be loose enough to be easily poured over the top of the cheesecake.

2. Remove the cake from the freezer and remove the plastic wrap. If the cheesecake has settled unevenly, you will need to trim off the top edges of the cake. Use a small, sharp paring knife to slice off as small an amount as necessary to create a completely even and flat top.

3. Pour the hot Lemon Curd onto the top of the frozen cake, swirling the cake pan around until the curd completely and evenly covers the top of the cake. Place the cake in the refrigerator for 1 hour, or until the Lemon Curd is completely firm.

SWISS MERINGUE

5 egg whites

1¾ cups granulated sugar

1. Combine the egg whites and sugar in a medium, heatproof mixing bowl set over a pan of simmering water (do not allow the bowl to touch the water). Cook, whisking continuously, until the mixture is hot to the touch and frothy, about 4 minutes. If you are using a candy thermometer, cook to 170°F.

2. Remove the bowl from over the water and transfer to a stand mixer fitted with the whisk attachment. Whip on high speed until cooled, glossy, and tripled in volume, about 6 minutes. The meringue should be made when ready to decorate the cake.

DECOR

1 recipe Swiss Meringue

Lemon slices or flower petals for garnish (optional)

Raspberry Sauce or Blackberry Sauce (pages 168–170) (optional)

1. Remove the lemon curd–topped cheesecake from the refrigerator and unmold from the pan (see page 14). Transfer the cheesecake to a clean 10-inch round cake board (optional) and place on a doily-covered 12-inch round cake board or directly onto a cake plate.

2. Fit a pastry bag with a ½-inch plain round decorating tip and fill with the Swiss Meringue. Working in a clockwise direction from the outside in, pipe individual peaked dollops of meringue over the top of the cake to completely cover the lemon curd. Using a propane torch, lightly burn the edges of the meringue until browned. (Some areas may be browned and others may have a hint of black.)

3. Defrost the decorated cheesecake in the refrigerator for 6 to 8 hours after adding the meringue. This cake can sit at room temperature for up to 1 hour before serving. If desired, decorate with lemon slices or flower petals. Serve slices with sauce, if desired.

Strawberry Poppy Seed Cake

For me, a fine poppy seed cake defines a great bakery. It is quite a triumph to devise one that is sufficiently sturdy to support the volume of poppy seeds while retaining a light and airy texture. Creamy, cakey, crunchy, and light, this is one of my all-time favorite creations. Because the strawberries play a key role, they must be very ripe and flavorful, so bake this in the summer, when juicy berries abound at farmers' markets.

The pastry cream requires the use of two different starches. Potato starch has a cleaner, less chalky flavor than cornstarch, and produces smoother results. It also can be cooked at a higher temperature, which is important when making custard. If you cannot find potato starch (often available in the kosher foods section of the super-market), replace it with extra cornstarch. Adding gelatin to the pastry cream is not optional, since it stabilizes the assembled torte. Without it, the layers might slide apart when cut and served.

LEMON POPPY SEED CAKE

MAKES ONE 10-INCH CAKE

SERVES 14 TO 16

1⅓ cups unsalted butter,
room temperature,
cut into ¼-inch cubes,
plus 2 teaspoons, melted
but not hot, for greasing pan

2¾ cups all-purpose flour

Pinch of salt

1 teaspoon baking powder

1⅓ cups granulated sugar

6 large eggs

Grated zest of 4 medium
lemons

Juice of 4 medium lemons,
strained

½ cup poppy seeds

1. Preheat the oven to 300°F. Grease the bottom and sides of a 10-by-3-inch round cake pan with removable bottom with the 2 teaspoons melted butter and line the bottom with a 10-inch-diameter parchment paper round.

2. Sift together the flour, salt, and baking powder and set aside.

3. In the bowl of a stand mixer fitted with the paddle attachment, beat together the sugar and cubed butter until light and fluffy, about 3 minutes. Add the eggs one at a time, mixing until well incorporated. Add the lemon zest and juice. Mix in the sifted ingredients in several additions until combined, scraping down the sides of the bowl as needed. Add the poppy seeds and mix just until blended. Be careful not to overmix, as the poppy seeds can cause the batter to change color.

4. Pour the batter into the prepared pan and place on a rack in the center of the oven. Bake until the top of the cake is slightly golden brown and a knife inserted into the center of the cake comes out clean, about 1 hour.

5. Remove the cake from the oven and allow to cool completely. Once cooled, remove the cake from the pan (see page 12) and peel the parchment paper from the bottom of the cake. Wrap the cake tightly in plastic wrap until ready to use. The Lemon Poppy Seed Cake can be stored for up to 1 day at room temperature or in the freezer for up to 1 week.

LEMON SIMPLE SYRUP

¼ cup granulated sugar

½ cup freshly squeezed
lemon juice, strained

1. Combine the sugar with ¼ cup water in a small, heavy saucepan over medium-high heat and bring to a boil, stirring occasionally. Remove from the heat, pour into a clean bowl, and allow to cool.

2. Once fully cooled, stir in the lemon juice until combined. The Lemon Simple Syrup will keep for up to 1 day in an airtight container in the refrigerator. However, the flavor might change if stored for a longer period of time.

VANILLA PASTRY CREAM

2¾ cups heavy cream

1 cup whole milk

½ vanilla bean, scraped
(see page 12)

½ cup granulated sugar

6 large egg yolks

2 tablespoons cornstarch

2 tablespoons potato starch

⅓ cup plus 1 tablespoon
unsalted butter, room
temperature, cut into
¼-inch cubes

4 gelatin sheets (see page 11)

1. Combine 1½ cups heavy cream, the milk, and vanilla bean seeds in a medium, heavy saucepan over medium-high heat and bring to a boil.

2. In a heatproof, nonreactive mixing bowl, whisk together the sugar, egg yolks, and both starches until well combined and smooth. While whisking continuously, slowly pour the warm cream mixture into the egg mixture and whisk until blended. Return all to the saucepan and continue to cook over medium heat, whisking continuously, until the mixture begins to boil and has thickened into a custard. Strain through a fine-mesh sieve into a clean, nonreactive mixing bowl and mix in 1 tablespoon butter until fully combined and smooth. Cover with plastic wrap pressed directly onto the surface of the custard. Cool in the refrigerator for 2 hours.

3. Once the custard has cooled and is ready to use, remove it from the refrigerator.

4. In the bowl of a stand mixer fitted with the whisk attachment, add the remaining 1¼ cups cream and whip until soft peaks form, about 1 minute. Hold in the refrigerator until ready to use.

5. Soften the gelatin sheets in 4 cups cool water for 5 minutes. Squeeze out the excess water, then melt the gelatin in a small saucepan over low heat until liquid.

6. In the bowl of a stand mixer fitted with either the whisk or the paddle attachment, add the cooled pastry cream and beat gently to loosen. Add the remaining ⅓ cup butter and mix until combined. While the machine is running, pour in the melted gelatin and mix until fully incorporated and smooth. Remove the bowl from the mixer. Using a rubber spatula, gently fold in the whipped cream until just combined. The Vanilla Pastry Cream is best when made the same day as assembling the cake.

3 cups heavy cream

¼ cup granulated sugar

Lemon Poppy Seed Cake, baked and cooled

1 recipe Lemon Simple Syrup

1 recipe Vanilla Pastry Cream

1 pint fresh strawberries (reserve 3 whole berries for Decor)

1. In the bowl of a stand mixer fitted with the whisk attachment, whip together the cream and sugar until stiff peaks form, 2 to 3 minutes. Fit a pastry bag with a ½-inch plain round decorating tip and fill with half of the whipped cream. Hold all in the refrigerator until ready to use.

2. Set aside 3 of the best-looking strawberries to be used in the final decor. Hull and cut all of the remaining strawberries into 10 to 12 pieces each (¼- to ½-inch cubes).

3. Place the unwrapped cake on a flat work surface. Using a long serrated knife, slice off the top ¼ inch to even out the top of the cake as necessary. Set the cut piece aside to be used later to edge the cake (see page 14). Slice the cake horizontally into 3 even layers.

4. Using a 10-inch round cake board as the bottom of a 10-by-3-inch round cake pan with removable bottom (see page 13), place 1 cake layer on the cake board, cut side up. Using a pastry brush, moisten the cake layer with one-third of the Lemon Simple Syrup.

5. Measure out ½ cup of the Vanilla Pastry Cream and set aside to be used on the top layer of the cake. Using an offset spatula, spread half of the remaining pastry cream evenly onto the syrup-soaked cake layer and sprinkle with half of the cut strawberries. Be sure to cover the entire cake surface evenly. Using the prepared pastry bag, pipe a layer of whipped cream in a spiral pattern over the strawberries, using the entire bag. Refill the bag with the remaining whipped cream to be used on the next layer.

6. Top with the second layer of cake and repeat with one-third of the syrup, the remaining pastry cream, and strawberries. Finish this layer with piped whipped cream.

7. Top with the final layer of cake, moisten with the remaining Lemon Simple Syrup, and cover with the reserved ½ cup of Vanilla Pastry Cream. Tightly wrap the cake in the pan in plastic wrap and place in the freezer overnight.

3 cups heavy cream

¼ cup granulated sugar

Toasted cake crumbs
(see page 14)

3 reserved strawberries,
stems on, sliced

1 lemon, sliced

Fresh rose petals (optional)

Strawberry Sauce
and/or Vanilla Sauce
(page 170) (optional)

1. Remove the assembled cake from the freezer, remove the plastic wrap, and unmold the cake from the pan (see page 14).

2. In the bowl of a stand mixer fitted with the whisk attachment, whip together the cream and sugar until stiff peaks form, 2 to 3 minutes. Fit a pastry bag with a ¼-inch, 7-point star decorating tip, fill with about 1 cup of the whipped cream, and set aside. Using an offset spatula, spread a ½-inch-thick layer of the remaining whipped cream around the sides and top of the cake as evenly as possible. Press the cake crumbs evenly around the sides of the cake to completely cover the whipped cream (see page 14).

3. Optional: Use a 16-portion cake marker to score the top of the cake into slices.

4. Using the prepared pastry bag, pipe 16 rosettes around the top edge of the cake, one on each marked slice. Return the decorated cake to the refrigerator to defrost overnight and allow all the fruit to thaw.

5. Before serving, place the cake on a doily-covered 12-inch round cake board or directly onto a cake plate. Slice each strawberry into quarters and pick the 8 best-looking pieces. Slice the lemon crosswise into 6 slices and then cut each slice in half. Pick the 8 most attractive slices.

6. Decorate each rosette with either a lemon or strawberry slice or a rose petal. This cake can be displayed for up to 1 hour at room temperature before serving. Serve slices with sauce, if desired.

Extraordinary
AUTUMN

Chocolate Tiramisù

Since few flavor combinations beat the pairing of coffee and chocolate, this twist on the perennially popular Italian dessert is packed with both. Chocolate Tiramisù pulls out all the stops by following each smooth, velvety bite with a bold espresso finish.

Note that Trablit coffee extract provides a flavor sufficiently strong to offset the creaminess of the mascarpone cheese. Though expensive and found mostly only online (see page 171), it is absolutely worth the investment. Similarly, choosing high-quality chocolates will significantly heighten the flavor.

It is imperative that the mascarpone be at room temperature in order to properly combine with the other ingredients in the mousse. Cold mascarpone will result in unappetizing lumps.

BITTERSWEET CHOCOLATE GÉNOISE

MAKES ONE 10-INCH CAKE | SERVES 16 TO 18   **(see page 67)**

ESPRESSO SIMPLE SYRUP

¾ cup granulated sugar

2 tablespoons instant espresso powder

1. Combine the sugar with ¾ cup water in a small, heavy saucepan over medium-high heat and bring to a boil, stirring occasionally. Remove from the heat and whisk in the espresso powder until fully dissolved and incorporated. Pour into a clean bowl and allow to cool.

2. Once fully cooled, stir in ¼ cup cold water to thin it out. The Espresso Simple Syrup will keep for up to 3 days in an airtight container in the refrigerator.

SEMISWEET CHOCOLATE GANACHE

(see page 85)

2½ cups heavy cream

5 ounces (¾ cup) milk chocolate, coarsely chopped

11 ounces (scant 2 cups) 64% semisweet chocolate, coarsely chopped

2 teaspoons Trablit coffee extract (see page 105)

1½ cups granulated sugar

6 large egg yolks

5 gelatin sheets (see page 11)

¾ cup mascarpone cheese, room temperature

1. In the bowl of a stand mixer fitted with the whisk attachment, whip the cream until soft peaks form, 2 to 3 minutes. Hold in the refrigerator until ready to use.

2. Melt both chocolates in a medium, heatproof mixing bowl set over a pan of simmering water (do not allow the bowl to touch the water), stirring occasionally. Stir in the coffee extract until well blended and smooth.

3. Combine the sugar with ⅓ cup plus 2 tablespoons water in a small, heavy saucepan over medium-high heat and bring to a boil. Insert a candy thermometer and cook to 230° to 240°F, the soft-ball stage.

4. While the sugar is cooking, place the egg yolks in the bowl of a stand mixer fitted with the whisk attachment and whip at medium-high speed until thick and light, about 3 minutes. Carefully pour the hot sugar syrup into the whipping yolks in a continuous stream, being careful to avoid pouring the syrup directly onto the moving whisk. Increase the mixer speed to high and whip until the mixture has cooled down and has tripled in volume, 7 to 10 minutes.

5. Soften the gelatin sheets in 6 cups cool water for 5 minutes. Squeeze out the excess water, then melt the gelatin in a small, heavy saucepan over low heat until liquid. Pour the gelatin into the whipping eggs and whip until combined. Reduce the mixer speed to medium or medium-high and add the melted warm chocolate in several additions to ensure proper emulsification. Mix until fully combined. Remove the bowl from the mixer.

6. Place the mascarpone in a medium mixing bowl and whisk quickly to loosen. Using a hand whisk, mix the chocolate-egg mixture into the mascarpone in 3 separate additions. The mixture should be smooth and creamy after each addition. Using a rubber spatula, gently fold in the whipped cream. The Chocolate Mascarpone Mousse should be made just before assembling the cake, as it is easiest to work with in its original soft puddinglike state.

ASSEMBLY

Bittersweet Chocolate Génoise, baked and cooled

1 recipe Espresso Simple Syrup

1¾ cups Semisweet Chocolate Ganache

1 recipe Chocolate Mascarpone Mousse

1. Place the unwrapped génoise on a flat work surface. Using a long serrated knife, slice off the top ¼ inch to even out the top of the cake as necessary. Set the cut piece aside to be used later as an option to edge the cake (see page 14). Slice the cake horizontally into three ¼-inch-thick layers.

2. Using a 10-inch round cake board as the bottom of a 10-by-3-inch round cake pan with removable bottom (see page 13), place 1 cake layer on the cake board, cut side up. Using a pastry brush, moisten the cake layer with one-third of the Espresso Simple Syrup.

3. Using an offset spatula, spread ½ cup Semisweet Chocolate Ganache evenly onto the syrup-soaked cake layer and cover with approximately half of the Chocolate Mascarpone Mousse.

4. Top with a second layer of génoise and repeat with one-third of the syrup, another ½ cup ganache, and the remaining Chocolate Mascarpone Mousse.

5. Top with the final layer of cake and moisten with the remaining Espresso Simple Syrup. Spread ¾ cup of Semisweet Chocolate Ganache as evenly and as smoothly as possible over the top of the cake. Tightly wrap the cake in the pan in plastic wrap and place in the freezer overnight.

DECOR

3 cups heavy cream

¼ cup granulated sugar

4 teaspoons Trablit coffee extract

About 2¾ cups Semisweet Chocolate Ganache, softened (see page 12)

Toasted chocolate cake crumbs (see page 14) or chocolate pailletes

6 to 8 chocolate-covered espresso beans

1. In the bowl of a stand mixer fitted with the whisk attachment, whip together the cream and sugar until stiff peaks form, 2 to 3 minutes. Remove the bowl from the mixer. Using a rubber spatula, fold in the coffee extract until the whipped cream is an even, light brown color. Fit a pastry bag with a ½-inch plain round decorating tip and fill with 2 cups of the coffee whipped cream. This will be used for the final Decor piped on top of the cake. Fit a second pastry bag with a ½-inch plain round decorating tip and fill with the ganache.

2. Remove the cake from the freezer, remove the plastic wrap, and unmold the cake from the pan (see page 14). Using an offset spatula, spread a thick layer of the remaining whipped cream (not in the pastry bag) around the sides and top of the cake as evenly as possible. Be sure to use up all of the remaining whipped cream to frost the cake with a thick, even layer. Press the toasted cake crumbs evenly onto the sides of the cake to completely cover the whipped cream (see page 14).

3. Using both pastry bags, pipe first the coffee whipped cream, then the Semisweet Chocolate Ganache (in alternating stripes across the top of the cake) (see photo). You should have approximately 7 whipped cream stripes and 6 ganache stripes. Top every other stripe with a chocolate-covered espresso bean. Return the decorated cake to the refrigerator and allow the cake to fully defrost for 6 hours before serving.

4. When ready to serve, remove the cake from the refrigerator and place on a doily-covered, 12-inch round cake board or directly onto a cake plate. The cake can sit at room temperature for up to 1 hour before slicing.

New York, New York

This apple-chocolate mousse cake is my pastry homage to the Big Apple. Bold and bittersweet chocolate mousse plays off a deliciously sweet, caramelized apple surprise that offers a bright, fresh flavor and prevents the cake from being overpowering. The touch of cinnamon and the richness of the mousse make this ideal for the later months of the year.

Because apples are not precisely uniform in size, it is hard to judge exactly how many are needed for the decor, and the amounts specified take into account bruising and errors in slicing. The most important detail is to cut the slices as uniformly as possible for a beautiful look.

When I make this cake, I like to decorate it with apple slices held in place by a satin ribbon. If you prefer, finish the cake by edging the sides with toasted cake crumbs, chocolate shavings or paillettes, or elegant store-bought cookies. Any of these would give a stylish finish and accent the flavors.

CHOCOLATE SOUR CREAM CAKE

MAKES ONE 10-INCH CAKE | SERVES 16 TO 20   (page 151)

RUM SIMPLE SYRUP

½ cup granulated sugar

⅓ cup Myer's dark rum

1. Combine the sugar with ½ cup water in a small, heavy saucepan over medium-high heat and bring to a boil, stirring occasionally. Remove from the heat, pour into a clean bowl, and allow to cool.

2. Once fully cooled, stir in the rum until combined. The Rum Simple Syrup will keep for up to 3 days in an airtight container in the refrigerator.

CARAMELIZED APPLES

3 ripe medium-large Golden Delicious apples

¼ cup granulated sugar

3 tablespoons unsalted butter, room temperature

1 teaspoon ground cinnamon

3 tablespoons Myer's dark rum

1. Peel, core, and cut the apples into ¼- to ½-inch cubes. In a medium-large sauté pan over medium heat, melt together the sugar, butter, and cinnamon. Stir in the cubed apples and cook, stirring continuously, until the apples begin to soften, about 4 minutes. Increase the heat to medium-high, add the rum, and continue cooking and stirring until the apples become soft, about 10 minutes.

2. Remove from the heat and transfer the cooked apple mixture to a clean container. Allow to cool to room temperature. Once fully cooled, the Caramelized Apples will keep for up to 2 days tightly covered in plastic wrap or in an airtight container in the refrigerator.

BITTERSWEET CHOCOLATE CHANTILLY

7 ounces (1⅓ cups) 70% bittersweet chocolate, coarsely chopped

3 cups heavy cream

2 tablespoons glucose or light corn syrup

2 tablespoons honey

1. Place the chocolate in a medium, heatproof mixing bowl.

2. Bring the cream, the glucose, and honey to a boil in a small, heavy saucepan over medium-high heat. Pour the hot cream mixture over the chocolate and let sit for 5 minutes. Using a rubber spatula, stir slowly and gently in a circular motion until mixture is fully combined and homogenous. Allow to cool slightly.

3. Cover with plastic and refrigerate overnight. The chantilly can be made up to 2 days in advance and stored in an airtight container in the refrigerator.

SEMISWEET CHOCOLATE GANACHE

(see page 42)

ASSEMBLY

1 recipe Bittersweet Chocolate Chantilly

Chocolate Sour Cream Cake, baked and cooled

1 recipe Rum Simple Syrup

1 recipe Semisweet Chocolate Ganache

1 recipe Caramelized Apples

1. In the bowl of a stand mixer fitted with the whisk attachment, whip the Bittersweet Chocolate Chantilly until stiff peaks form, 2 minutes.

2. Place the unwrapped cake on a flat work surface. Using a long serrated knife, slice off the top ¼ inch to even out the top of the cake as necessary. Slice the cake horizontally into 3 even layers.

3. Using a 10-inch round cake board as the bottom of a 10-by-3-inch round cake pan with removable bottom (see page 13), place 1 cake layer on the cake board, cut side up. Brush the cake layer with one-third of the Rum Simple Syrup.

4. Using an offset spatula, spread 1 cup of cooled ganache evenly over the syrup-soaked cake layer and cover with half of the whipped chantilly. Sprinkle half of the apples over the chantilly layer.

5. Top with a second layer of cake and repeat with another one-third of the simple syrup, 1 cup ganache, remaining chantilly, and the rest of the apples.

6. Top with the final layer of cake, moisten with the remaining simple syrup, and cover evenly with the remaining ganache. Tightly wrap the pan in plastic and place in the freezer overnight.

SEMISWEET CHOCOLATE GLAZE

2 tablespoons
granulated sugar

6 ounces (1 cup) 56% to
58% semisweet chocolate,
coarsely chopped

3 tablespoons grapeseed
or vegetable oil

⅓ cup heavy cream

1 tablespoon glucose
or light corn syrup

1. Combine the sugar with 2 tablespoons water in a small, heavy saucepan over medium-high heat and bring to a boil, stirring occasionally. Set aside.

2. Melt the chocolate in a medium, heatproof mixing bowl set over a pan of simmering water (do not allow the bowl to touch the water), stirring occasionally. Remove the bowl from over the water. Pour the oil into the melted chocolate and stir until smooth and homogenous.

3. Mix the cream and glucose into the sugar syrup, place over medium-high heat, and bring to a boil.

4. Slowly whisk the hot cream-sugar mixture into the melted, warm chocolate in several additions. Whisk until smooth and glossy. Strain through a medium-mesh sieve into a clean bowl. The Semisweet Chocolate Glaze is best made when ready to glaze the cake.

DECOR

1 recipe Semisweet
Chocolate Glaze, warm

3 ripe medium-large
Golden Delicious apples

1 tablespoon freshly
squeezed lemon juice

1 to 1½ yards of ¼-inch
brown satin ribbon
(depending on whether
or not you are going
to tie a bow)

1 floral pin or pearlhead
pin (optional)

Caramel Sauce or
Chocolate Sauce
(page 168 or 169)
(optional)

1. Remove the assembled cake from the freezer, remove the plastic wrap, and unmold the cake from the pan (see page 14). Place the frozen cake on a wire cooling rack set over a baking sheet. Pour the warm chocolate glaze generously over the frozen cake, using a metal spatula to spread the glaze smoothly and evenly over the top and sides, dipping the spatula in hot water and then quickly gliding it over the glaze. The top should look very smooth and finished. The sides are not as important because the bottom 2 inches will be covered with sliced apples. Place the cake on a doily-covered 12-inch round cake board or onto a cake plate.

2. Cut each apple in half. Next, slice eight ⅛-inch-thick slices from each half. Using a pastry brush, lightly coat each apple slice with lemon juice to keep them from turning brown. One at a time, place the apple slices vertically onto and around the sides of the cake. The bottom of each apple slice should line up with the bottom edge of the cake, and each slice should stick easily onto the moist glaze. It is important that you place each apple slice barely overlapping the next so that they do not pop off of the cake. You will be tying a ribbon around all of the apples, which will help stabilize the slices and prevent them from falling off.

3. Measure the ribbon so that it is long enough to fit around the cake with plenty of ribbon to create a bow (it is like tying a shoelace). The ribbon can be centered halfway up the cake or around the bottom, according to your preference. An option is to create a bow and tie it in the center or simply wrap the ribbon around the cake and pin it in place without a bow. Once all of the apple slices have been added, wrap the ribbon around the side of the cake, over the apples, tying a bow in the front center.

4. Allow the decorated cake to fully defrost in the refrigerator for 6 to 8 hours. Remove the cake from the refrigerator and let sit at room temperature for 1 hour before serving. Serve slices with sauce, if desired.

Banana Cream Torte

GLUTEN-FREE

Baking has changed greatly since I was a kid. The number of people with dietary restrictions such as wheat sensitivity and gluten intolerance has inspired chefs to adapt recipes for standard cakes. My number-one challenge: making a gluten-free cake that is as decadent and extraordinary as my other desserts.

This delicious, moist, dense banana cake is studded with chopped bananas and loaded with flavor. As a substitute for wheat flour, brown rice flour is combined with almond flour to impart great texture.

To elevate it beyond an ordinary cake, I created a unique torte enhanced by pecan dacquoise, a departure from tradition that adds a crunchy texture and toasted flavor. (A dacquoise is a nut-flavored baked meringue.) Inspired by carrot cake, the torte is layered and covered with a rich cream cheese frosting.

Because this cake is so dense, it may take longer to bake and rise to a lesser height than you expect. However, once baked, it will retain its moisture thanks to both the fruit and the fat in the almond flour.

BANANA CAKE

MAKES ONE 10-INCH CAKE

SERVES 16 TO 18

⅓ cup unsalted butter, room temperature, cut into ¼-inch cubes, plus 2 teaspoons, melted but not hot, for greasing pan

1 cup honey

4 large eggs

2 large ripe bananas, coarsely chopped

¾ cup drained and diced canned pineapple

¾ cup finely chopped pecans

1 tablespoon potato flour

2 tablespoons coconut flour

1½ cups brown rice flour

2½ cups almond flour

½ teaspoon baking soda

1½ teaspoons ground cinnamon

½ teaspoon ground nutmeg

½ teaspoon ground cloves

½ teaspoon ground cardamom

1. Preheat the oven to 300°F. Butter the bottom and sides of a 10-by-3-inch round cake pan with removable bottom with the 2 teaspoons melted butter and line the bottom with a 10-inch-diameter parchment paper round.

2. In the bowl of a stand mixer fitted with the paddle attachment, beat together the remaining butter and the honey until very well combined, about 2 minutes. Add the eggs and mix until combined.

3. In the bowl of a food processor fitted with the blade attachment, blend the bananas until mushy. Pour into a clean mixing bowl and stir in the pineapple and pecans.

4. Sift together all of the flours and dry ingredients. Remove the batter from the mixer. Using a rubber spatula, fold in the sifted dry ingredients until well combined. Then fold in the fruit and nuts.

5. Pour the batter into the prepared cake pan and place on a rack in the center of the oven. Bake until browned, firm to the touch, and the blade of an inserted knife comes out clean but moist, about 90 minutes.

6. Remove the cake from the oven and cool completely. Once cooled, remove the cake from the pan (see page 12) and peel the parchment paper from the bottom of the cake. Wrap the cake tightly in plastic wrap until ready to use. This Banana Cake can only be stored at room temperature for up to 24 hours before it begins to lose moistness.

VANILLA SIMPLE SYRUP

½ cup granulated sugar

2 tablespoons vanilla extract

1. Combine the sugar with ½ cup water in a small, heavy saucepan over medium-high heat and bring to a boil, stirring occasionally. Remove from the heat, pour into a clean bowl, and allow to cool.

2. Once fully cooled, stir in the vanilla until combined. The Vanilla Simple Syrup will keep for up to 3 days in an airtight container in the refrigerator.

CREAM CHEESE FROSTING

1 cup unsalted butter, room temperature, cut into ¼-inch cubes

4 cups powdered sugar, sifted

2 teaspoons vanilla extract

2 (8-ounce) packages (2 cups) cream cheese, room temperature

1. In the bowl of a stand mixer fitted with the paddle attachment, beat together the butter and powdered sugar until smooth and somewhat fluffy, about 3 minutes. Add the vanilla and then the cream cheese, mixing until well combined.

2. Remove the bowl from the mixer. Measure out 5 cups of frosting, to be used in assembling the cake, and set aside. The remaining 2 cups will be used to decorate the cake. The Cream Cheese Frosting will keep for up to 3 days in an airtight container in the refrigerator but must be brought to room temperature before using so that it is soft enough to spread easily.

PECAN DACQUOISE

2 teaspoons unsalted butter, melted but not hot

¼ cup pecan pieces, toasted and cooled (see page 12)

⅔ cup sliced almonds, skin on, toasted and cooled (see page 12)

1 teaspoon arrowroot or cornstarch

3 large egg whites

¼ cup granulated sugar

1. Preheat the oven to 250°F. Using a pencil, trace a 9-inch-diameter circle onto a sheet of parchment paper. Flip the paper over, pencil side down, onto a baking sheet. Using a pastry brush, coat the traced circle with the melted butter.

2. In the bowl of a food processor fitted with the blade attachment, finely grind together the pecans, almonds, and arrowroot.

3. In the bowl of a stand mixer fitted with the whisk attachment, whip the egg whites on medium speed for 2 minutes. When the egg whites are frothy, begin to slowly add the sugar and increase the speed to medium-high. Whip until the egg whites are stiff but still have a creamy texture, about 3 minutes. Remove the bowl from the mixer.

4. Using a rubber spatula, carefully fold the processed nut mixture into the meringue until well combined. Fit a pastry bag with a ½-inch plain round decorating tip and fill with dacquoise batter. Starting in the center of the traced outline on the sheet of parchment paper and working in a counter-clockwise direction, pipe a spiral to completely fill in the 9-inch circle.

5. Place the baking sheet on a rack in the center of the oven and bake until the dacquoise is crisp, dry to the touch, and lightly browned, about 90 minutes.

6. The Pecan Dacquoise can be made 1 to 2 days in advance if stored uncovered in a dry place, like a cool oven. If the dacquoise softens up while stored, warm it in a 250°F oven for 5 minutes. It should crisp up again once cooled.

2 ripe medium bananas, preferably without brown spots

1 teaspoon freshly squeezed lemon juice

2 cups heavy cream

1 tablespoon granulated sugar

5 cups Cream Cheese Frosting, room temperature

Banana Cake, baked and cooled

1 recipe Vanilla Simple Syrup

Pecan Dacquoise, baked and cooled

2 tablespoons apricot jam

1. Peel the bananas and slice into ¼-inch-thick rounds. Cut each round in half. Sprinkle the banana slices with lemon juice to keep from turning brown.

2. In the bowl of a stand mixer fitted with the whisk attachment, whip together the heavy cream and sugar until stiff peaks form, 2 minutes. Remove the bowl from the mixer. Using a rubber spatula, fold the whipped cream into the Cream Cheese Frosting until well combined.

3. Place the unwrapped Banana Cake on a flat work surface. Using a long serrated knife, slice off the top ¼ inch to even out the top of the cake as necessary. Slice the cake horizontally into 3 even layers.

4. Using a 10-inch round cake board as the bottom of a 10-by-3-inch round cake pan with removable bottom (see page 13), place 1 cake layer on the cake board, cut side up. Using a pastry brush, moisten the cake layer with one-third of the Vanilla Simple Syrup.

5. Using an offset spatula, spread about 3 cups of the Cream Cheese Frosting–flavored whipped cream evenly onto the syrup-soaked cake layer. Sprinkle half the banana slices evenly over the entire layer and drizzle with half of the apricot jam.

6. Place the Pecan Dacquoise, spiral side down, firmly on top of the bananas and press down lightly to adhere. Evenly cover the dacquoise with approximately 1 cup of the Cream Cheese Frosting–flavored whipped cream.

7. Top with a second layer of cake, cut side up, and moisten with another one-third of the Vanilla Simple Syrup. Repeat layering with another 3 cups of the frosting-flavored whipped cream, the remaining bananas, and the rest of the apricot jam.

8. Top with the final layer of cake, moisten with the remaining simple syrup, and evenly spread the remaining Cream Cheese Frosting–flavored whipped cream, about 1½ cups, over the top of the cake until smooth. Tightly wrap the cake in the pan in plastic wrap and place in the freezer overnight.

2 cups heavy cream

1 tablespoon granulated sugar

2 cups Cream Cheese
Frosting, room temperature

1 cup sliced almonds,
toasted and cooled

1 small to medium ripe banana

2 large roses (optional)

Caramel Sauce and Passion
Fruit Sauce or Vanilla Sauce
(pages 168, 169, or 170)
(optional)

1. In the bowl of a stand mixer fitted with the whisk attachment, whip together the heavy cream and sugar until stiff peaks form, 2 minutes. Remove the bowl from the mixer. Using a rubber spatula, fold the whipped cream into the Cream Cheese Frosting until well combined. Fit a pastry bag with a ½-inch, 9-point closed star tip and fill with half of the Cream Cheese Frosting–flavored whipped cream.

2. Remove the assembled cake from the freezer, remove the plastic wrap, and unmold the cake from the pan (see page 14). Using an offset spatula, spread the remaining Cream Cheese Frosting–flavored whipped cream evenly over the top and sides of the cake. Press the almonds evenly around the sides of the cake to completely cover the frosting-flavored whipped cream (see page 14).

3. Using the prepared pastry bag, pipe large frosting-flavored whipped cream rosettes in a swirling pattern over the top of the cake. Place the decorated cake in the refrigerator for 6 hours to completely thaw.

4. Allow the cake to sit at room temperature for 1 hour before serving. Immediately before serving, peel the banana and cut into ⅛-inch-thick slices. Top each rosette with a banana slice and scatter rose petals over the top of the cake. Serve slices with sauce, if desired.

Yuzu Tea Cakes

Deliciously moist with a hint of tartness and crunch, these elegant little tea cakes are an adaptation of classic French *financiers*, traditionally baked in rectangular molds that mimic the shapes of gold ingots. The idea of adding yuzu as a flavoring came to me in Japan, where the sour citrus fruit is a prominent ingredient in pastries.

Bottled yuzu juice can be found in most Asian grocery stores or online. Similar in flavor to lemon juice, it also hints at mandarin orange and salt. If desired, substitute lemon juice and curd as needed.

Given the high butter content, the cakes taste best served straight from the oven, and are spectacular when garnished with warm sautéed berries and whipped cream. Because financier batter is denser and richer than cupcake batter, it is not necessary to fill the baking molds all the way to the top. You will need special paper baking cups (3⅛-by-1⁹⁄₁₆-by-1⅝-inch; see page 9) to bake these individual cakes. These baking cups are easy to use and bake a perfect, moist product with no buttering or cleanup. Just peel the cakes out of their cups after baking and serve. The cakes can also be baked in small boat-shaped molds or mini-muffin pans.

YUZU CURD

MAKES 10 INDIVIDUAL CAKES

SERVES 10

2 large eggs

½ cup granulated sugar

Grated zest of 2 lemons

Grated zest of ½ orange

¼ cup freshly squeezed lime juice

1 tablespoon yuzu juice

¼ cup unsalted butter, room temperature, cut into ¼-inch cubes

1. Combine the first 6 ingredients in a heatproof, nonreactive mixing bowl set over a pan of simmering water (do not allow the bowl to touch the water). Cook, whisking continuously, until the mixture is frothy and begins to thicken to a custard, about 4 minutes. If using a candy thermometer, cook to 190°F.

2. Remove the bowl from over the water and whisk in the butter until fully combined. The curd should be smooth and homogenous. Strain through a fine-mesh sieve into a clean, nonreactive mixing bowl. Cover with plastic wrap pressed directly onto the surface of the curd. Cool in the refrigerator until ready to use or for up to 3 days.

YUZU ALMONDS

⅓ cup plus 1 tablespoon granulated sugar

1 cup sliced raw almonds

2 tablespoons yuzu juice

1. Combine the sugar with ⅓ cup water in a small, heavy saucepan over medium-high heat and bring to a boil. Remove from the heat, pour into a heatproof, nonreactive mixing bowl, and allow to cool completely.

2. Once fully cooled, mix in the almonds and yuzu juice until well coated and combined. Let sit at room temperature for a minimum of 30 minutes or up to 2 hours before using.

YUZU TEA CAKES

¾ cup unsalted butter, room temperature, cut into ¼-inch cubes

1½ cups almond flour, loosely packed

1 cup plus 2 tablespoons all-purpose flour

3 cups powdered sugar, sifted

7 large egg whites

1 recipe Yuzu Curd

1 recipe Yuzu Almonds, drained

Whipped cream (optional)

1. Preheat the oven to 325°F. Place ten 3⅛-by-1⁹⁄₁₆-by-1⅝-inch individual rectangular paper baking cups on a baking sheet.

2. Heat the butter in a small, heavy sauté pan over medium-low heat. Allow the butter to melt and then come to a boil. Continue boiling over medium heat, swirling the pan every 30 seconds, until the butter becomes frothy and begins to brown, about 4 minutes. Remove from the heat and strain through a fine-mesh sieve into a clean bowl.

3. Combine both flours and 2¾ cups powdered sugar in the bowl of a food processor fitted with the blade attachment and pulse until fine. Transfer the ground mixture to a large mixing bowl. Using a whisk stir the egg whites directly into the flour mixture in 2 additions, until the whites are fully combined and mixture has achieved a batterlike consistency. Pour the browned butter into the batter in 3 additions, mixing well after each addition to fully incorporate all of the browned butter.

4. Place ⅓ cup of the tea cake batter into each baking cup. Top each with approximately 1 generous tablespoon of the Yuzu Curd. Evenly divide any remaining Yuzu Curd among the cakes. Using the stem of a fork, swirl the batter and curd together, creating a marbled effect. Sprinkle the Yuzu Almonds evenly over the tea cakes.

5. Place the cakes on a rack in the center of the oven and bake until the almond topping is slightly brown and firm to the touch, about 35 minutes. The blade of a knife should come out clean when inserted into the center of the cakes. The Yuzu Curd may still be semi-soft and bubbly, but when the cake cools, it will firm up and be presentable.

6. Remove the cakes from the oven and allow to cool for 30 minutes. Once cooled, peel off the paper baking cup from each cake. Fill a small sieve with the remaining powdered sugar and sprinkle over each cake. Arrange cakes on a serving platter.

7. Serve with whipped cream, if desired.

Tortamisù

Because I enjoy the flavor of dark-roast Italian coffee, traditional Italian tiramisù is one of my favorite desserts. I love the way creamy mascarpone tempers the acidic coffee. By layering the ingredients cake-style, I reinterpreted this classic, thus making it easier to serve. Ultracreamy yet light, Tortamisù is an out-of-this-world treat for coffee lovers.

The Ricotta Pound Cake recipe makes a very porous cake, so moisten it with warm espresso-style coffee soon after it leaves the oven. This allows you to add the exact amount you desire. I sometimes use chocolate paillettes (see page 171) to rim the side for a more elegant look. However, toasted cake crumbs or store-bought ladyfingers are other great options. It is imperative that the marscapone be at room temperature in order to properly combine with the other ingredients in the mousse.

RICOTTA POUND CAKE

MAKES ONE 10-INCH CAKE | SERVES 14 TO 16   (see page 57)

MASCARPONE MOUSSE

2 gelatin sheets (see page 11)

2 cups heavy cream

5 large egg yolks

½ cup granulated sugar

1½ cups mascarpone cheese, room temperature

1. Soften the gelatin sheets in 2 cups cool water for at least 5 minutes.

2. Bring the cream to a boil in a medium, heavy saucepan over medium-high heat.

3. Whisk together the egg yolks and sugar in a heatproof, nonreactive mixing bowl until blended. While whisking continuously, slowly pour the hot cream into the yolk mixture in several additions, incorporating fully after each addition. Pour the mixture back into the saucepan and cook over medium-high heat, stirring continuously in a back and forth motion with a heat-resistant spatula, as the mixture begins to thicken. Cook until the mixture is thick enough to coat the back of a spoon, about 5 minutes. Squeeze out the excess water from the softened gelatin and stir it into the warm custard until fully dissolved and the custard is smooth. Pour the custard through a fine-mesh sieve into a clean bowl. Cover with plastic wrap pressed directly onto the top of the custard and allow to cool to room temperature.

4. Place the mascarpone in a medium mixing bowl and whisk to loosen. Using a rubber spatula, fold the cooled custard into the mascarpone in several additions, until smooth and creamy. The Mascarpone Mousse should be made when you are ready to assemble the cake due to the gelatin content, which will render it too stiff to use if kept overnight or longer.

3 cups heavy cream

¼ cup granulated sugar

Ricotta Pound Cake, baked and cooled

2 cups warm espresso coffee

1 recipe Mascarpone Mousse

1. In the bowl of a stand mixer fitted with the whisk attachment, whip together the cream and sugar until stiff peaks form, 2 to 3 minutes. Fit a pastry bag with a ½-inch plain round decorating tip and fill with the whipped cream.

2. Place the unwrapped pound cake on a flat work surface. Using a long serrated knife, slice off the top ¼ inch to even out the top of the cake as necessary. Set the cut piece aside to be used later as an option to edge the cake (see page 14). Slice the cake horizontally into 3 even layers.

3. Using a 10-inch round cake board as the bottom of a 10-by-3-inch round cake pan with removable bottom (see page 13), place 1 cake layer on the cake board, cut side up. Using a pastry brush, moisten the cake layer with approximately one-third of the espresso coffee.

4. Using an offset spatula, spread half of the Mascarpone Mousse onto the espresso-soaked cake layer. Using the prepared pastry bag, pipe half of the whipped cream in a spiral pattern over the Mascarpone Mousse to cover.

5. Top with a second layer of cake and repeat with another one-third of the espresso, the remaining Mascarpone Mousse, and the rest of the whipped cream.

6. Top with the final layer of cake and moisten with the remaining espresso. Tightly wrap the assembled cake in plastic wrap and place in the freezer overnight.

3 cups heavy cream

¼ cup granulated sugar

1 cup chocolate paillettes
or toasted cake crumbs
(see page 14)

2 tablespoons cocoa powder

Additional rose petals
for decor (optional)

Chocolate Sauce and Vanilla
Sauce (page 169 and 170)
(optional)

1. Remove the assembled cake from the freezer, remove the plastic wrap, and unmold the cake from the pan (see page 14).

2. In the bowl of a stand mixer fitted with the whisk attachment, whip together the cream and sugar until stiff peaks form, 2 to 3 minutes. Fit a pastry bag with a ½-inch, 8-point open star decorating tip and fill with approximately one-third of the whipped cream. Set aside until ready to use.

3. Using an offset spatula, spread a ¼-inch-thick layer of the remaining whipped cream around the sides and top of the cake as evenly as possible. Edge with chocolate paillettes or press the toasted cake crumbs evenly around the sides of the cake to completely cover the whipped cream (see page 14).

4. Using the prepared pastry bag and working from the outside edge of the cake toward the center, pipe whipped cream in concentric circles over the top of the cake to completely cover. Fill a small sieve with the cocoa powder and lightly dust the top of the cake.

5. Place the cake on a doily-covered, 12-inch round cake board or directly onto a cake plate. Allow the cake to defrost in the refrigerator for 6 to 8 hours or overnight. Sprinkle fresh flower petals around the base of the cake, if desired. This cake can be displayed at room temperature for up to 1 hour before serving, but is best when served cold. Serve slices with sauce, if desired.

Blackberry Cheesecakes

This recipe was created after a summertime visit to my mother and stepfather's home on Vashon Island in the Pacific Northwest. The blackberries grew everywhere, and our mouths and hands were purple from picking and eating them fresh off the bushes. We had so many that we added them to every dessert we could think of, made jams and jellies, created unique cocktails, and whipped them into smoothies. The addicting combination of cream cheese and blackberry jam on bagels sparked the idea for these delectable desserts.

While not designed as a traditional sour cream–topped cheesecake, the fine layer on top adds a special note. The season in which you make this recipe will determine whether you use fresh berries for the decor or a beautiful dark glaze confected from frozen berries.

PECAN GRAHAM CRACKER CRUST

MAKES EIGHT 4-INCH
INDIVIDUAL CHEESECAKES

SERVES 8

¼ cup unsalted butter,
melted and warm,
plus 2 teaspoons, for
greasing pan

1 sleeve graham crackers,
finely ground in a food
processor

⅓ cup pecans, toasted
and cooled

⅓ cup (lightly packed)
brown sugar

1. Preheat the oven to 350°F. Grease the bottom and sides of eight 4-inch round springform cake pans with 2 teaspoons of the melted butter.

2. In the bowl of a food processor fitted with the blade attachment, pulse together the graham crackers and pecans to a coarse texture. Be careful not to overprocess or the oil from the nuts will cause the mixture to become wet and clump. Transfer the mixture to a clean mixing bowl and add the brown sugar. Using a rubber spatula, stir in the remaining ¼ cup melted butter, making sure that the butter is well incorporated and the crust is evenly moist throughout.

3. Measure ¼ cup of the crust mixture into each individual springform pan and using a curved spatula or a fork, flatten the crust and pack it tightly into the bottom of each pan (distribute any extra crust evenly among the pans).

4. Place the pans on a rack in the center of the oven and bake until the crust is lightly toasted in appearance, about 15 minutes.

5. Remove the pans from the oven and allow to cool completely. Once cooled, wrap each pan tightly in plastic wrap until ready to use. The baked Pecan Graham Cracker Crusts can be stored for up to 2 days in a dry, cool oven.

BLACKBERRY CHEESECAKES

24 fresh or frozen (but
not thawed) blackberries

2 tablespoons
blackberry jam

4 (8-ounce) packages
(4 cups) cream cheese,
room temperature

1 cup granulated sugar

4 large eggs

2 teaspoons vanilla extract

1 cup sour cream,
room temperature

1. Preheat the oven to 225°F.

2. In a small mixing bowl, combine the blackberries with the blackberry jam and set aside.

3. In the bowl of a stand mixer fitted with the paddle attachment, beat together the cream cheese and sugar on medium-high speed until light and fluffy, about 6 minutes. Using a rubber spatula, scrape down the sides of the mixing bowl. Reduce the mixer speed to low and add the eggs, one at a time. Scrape down the sides of the bowl as necessary and add the vanilla and sour cream. Remove the bowl from the mixer.

4. Divide the batter evenly among the 8 pans of baked crust. There should be ¾ to 1 cup of cheesecake batter per pan. Divide any excess batter evenly among the pans. Place 3 blackberries in the center of each cheesecake. Press the blackberries down so that they are completely covered by the batter.

5. Place the pans on a rack in the center of the oven and bake until the cheesecakes are lightly colored and the centers still jiggle slightly when touched, about 1 hour.

6. Remove the cheesecakes from the oven and allow to cool completely before adding the Sour Cream Topping.

SOUR CREAM TOPPING

1 cup sour cream,
room temperature

¼ cup granulated sugar

1 teaspoon vanilla extract

1. Combine all the ingredients in a medium mixing bowl. Using a rubber spatula, stir until blended.

2. Using a small offset spatula, spread approximately 3 tablespoons Sour Cream Topping over the top of each baked and cooled cheesecake, smoothing evenly.

3. Loosely wrap the cakes in their pans in plastic wrap and refrigerate overnight to set. At this point, the cheesecakes can be stored in the refrigerator for up to 24 hours. However, if finishing with the Blackberry Mirroir (Decor Option 2), freeze the cheesecakes overnight so that the top of each cake is a really hard surface onto which to pour the hot mirroir topping.

4 to 5 pints fresh
blackberries

¼ cup blackberry
preserves, strained

Blackberry Sauce
(page 168)

1. Remove the cheesecakes from the refrigerator, remove the plastic wrap, and unmold each cheesecake from its pan (see page 14).

2. Top each cheesecake with fresh blackberries to cover the sour cream layer completely. Drizzle each with approximately 2 teaspoons of preserves.

3. Return the cheesecakes to the refrigerator until serving. Blackberry Cheesecakes can be displayed at room temperature for up to 1 hour before serving. Serve with sauce.

DECOR OPTION 2

1 recipe Blackberry Mirroir
(page 54)

8 fresh blackberries or other
fresh berries of your choice

Blackberry Sauce
(page 168)

1. Remove the cheesecakes from the freezer and remove the plastic wrap. Spoon 2 tablespoons of hot Blackberry Mirroir onto the top of each cheesecake, swirling the cake pan around so that mirroir covers the sour cream layer completely. When all 8 cheesecakes are covered, place them in the refrigerator for a minimum of 4 hours. This will allow the mirroir to set on the top and the interior of each cheesecake to fully defrost.

2. When the mirroir is set, unmold the cheesecakes from the pans (see page 14). Top each cheesecake with 1 fresh blackberry or your choice of fresh berries. The Blackberry Cheesecakes can be stored in the refrigerator for up to 24 hours with the Blackberry Mirroir and can be taken out of the refrigerator up to 1 hour before serving. Serve with sauce.

Blood Orange Ricotta Cake

Every year I try to bring something fresh and unique to my family's traditional Thanksgiving spread. Light, refreshing, and loaded with flavor, this cake takes advantage of the wonderful combination of citrus and cranberry that is such a favorite of the season.

If you don't like cranberries, replace the cranberry jam with high-quality, purchased raspberry preserves. It is, however, necessary to use blood orange concentrate (see page 171). Blood orange juice is not a good substitute, since it lacks the intense flavor of the concentrate.

While there are many steps to making this cake, they all are very straightforward, and the decor is fairly simple. It is important to use a cake pan slightly larger than the diameter of the baked layers when assembling the cake. When you remove the assembled cake from the pan, the sides may be very soft, which can create an imperfect look. If necessary, use ladyfingers or toasted cake crumbs to edge the sides, both to enhance the appearance and to hide any imperfections.

RICOTTA POUND CAKE

MAKES ONE 10-INCH CAKE

SERVES 16 TO 18

2 teaspoons unsalted butter, melted but not hot

4 large eggs

1½ cups granulated sugar

¾ cup grapeseed or vegetable oil

¾ cup whole or skim-milk ricotta

2 teaspoons freshly squeezed orange juice, strained

½ teaspoon vanilla extract

2 cups all-purpose flour

2 teaspoons baking powder

1. Preheat the oven to 300°F. Butter the bottom and sides of a 9-by-3-inch round cake pan with removable bottom with the melted butter and line the bottom with a 9-inch-diameter parchment paper round.

2. In the bowl of a stand mixer fitted with the whisk attachment, whip together the eggs and sugar at medium-high speed until the mixture is very thick and falls in heavy ribbons, about 7 minutes.

3. In a separate bowl, whisk together the oil, ricotta, orange juice, and vanilla. Gently add the ricotta mixture to the egg mixture and whip just until blended.

4. Sift together the flour and baking powder. Add the sifted ingredients to the batter, mixing just until incorporated, scraping down the sides of the bowl as needed. Do not overmix. If necessary, finish folding in the sifted ingredients by hand, using a rubber spatula.

5. Pour the batter into the prepared cake pan and place on a rack in the center of the oven. Bake the cake until lightly browned on top, about 70 minutes. The cake is done when a knife blade inserted into the center comes out clean and when the top of the cake springs back lightly when touched.

6. Remove the cake from the oven and allow to cool completely. Once cooled, remove the cake from the pan (see page 12) and peel the parchment paper from the bottom of the cake. Wrap the cake tightly in plastic wrap until ready to use. The Ricotta Pound Cake can be stored for up to 1 day at room temperature or in the freezer for up to 1 week.

BLOOD ORANGE SIMPLE SYRUP

⅓ cup granulated sugar

½ cup blood orange concentrate

1. Combine the sugar with ⅓ cup water in a small, heavy saucepan over medium-high heat and bring to a boil, stirring occasionally. Remove from the heat, pour into a clean bowl, and allow to cool.

2. Once fully cooled, stir in the blood orange concentrate until combined. The Blood Orange Simple Syrup will keep for up to 1 day in an airtight container in the refrigerator.

BLOOD ORANGE CURD

1 gelatin sheet (see page 11)

4 large eggs

4 large egg yolks

½ cup granulated sugar

⅓ cup blood orange concentrate

⅓ cup freshly squeezed lemon juice

⅔ cup unsalted butter, room temperature, cut into ¼-inch cubes

1. Soften the gelatin sheet in 2 cups cool water for 3 minutes.

2. Combine the whole eggs, egg yolks, sugar, and both juices in a heatproof, nonreactive mixing bowl set over a pan of simmering water (do not allow the bowl to touch the water) and whisk together until the sugar begins to dissolve. Cook, whisking continuously, until the mixture begins to thicken to a custard, 5 to 7 minutes. If using a candy thermometer, cook to 170° to 180°F. Whisk in the butter. The curd should be smooth and homogenous.

3. Squeeze out the excess water from the gelatin and whisk the gelatin into the hot mixture until fully dissolved and combined. Remove the bowl from over the water and strain the curd through a medium-mesh sieve into a clean, nonreactive mixing bowl. Cover with plastic wrap pressed directly onto the surface of the curd and allow to cool in the refrigerator. The Blood Orange Curd can be stored for up to 3 days in an airtight container in the refrigerator.

CRANBERRY ORANGE PRESERVES

2 cups whole frozen cranberries

½ cup freshly squeezed orange juice, strained

¼ cup light corn syrup

½ cup granulated sugar

1. In the bowl of a food processor fitted with the blade attachment, pulse together the cranberries and the orange juice. The cranberries should still be in chunky pieces.

2. Combine the cranberry mixture with the corn syrup and sugar in a medium saucepan over medium-low heat. Stirring every 5 minutes, cook the mixture until it boils and thickens, 15 to 20 minutes. If using a candy thermometer, cook to approximately 210°F.

3. Transfer to a clean bowl. Cover with plastic wrap and cool in the refrigerator. The Cranberry Orange Preserves can be made up to 3 days in advance and stored in an airtight container in the refrigerator.

BLOOD ORANGE WHIPPED CREAM

4 cups heavy cream

Scant ½ cup granulated sugar

1 recipe Blood Orange Curd

In the bowl of a stand mixer fitted with the whisk attachment, whip together the cream and sugar until stiff peaks form, about 3 minutes. Remove the bowl from the mixer. Using a rubber spatula, fold in the Blood Orange Curd until combined, being careful not to overmix, which could make the stiffened whipped cream weak. The Blood Orange Whipped Cream should be made when ready to assemble the cake.

ASSEMBLY

1 pint fresh raspberries

1 recipe Cranberry Orange Preserves

Ricotta Pound Cake, baked and cooled

1 recipe Blood Orange Simple Syrup

1 recipe Blood Orange Whipped Cream

1. In a small mixing bowl, gently fold together the raspberries and the Cranberry Orange Preserves until combined.

2. Place the unwrapped pound cake on a flat work surface. Using a long serrated knife, slice off the top ¼ inch to even out the top of the cake as necessary. Slice the cake horizontally into 3 even layers.

3. Using a 10-inch round cake board as the bottom of a 10-by-3-inch round cake pan with removable bottom (see page 13), center 1 cake layer on the cake board, cut side up. Using a pastry brush, moisten the cake layer with one-third of the Blood Orange Simple Syrup.

4. Measure out 1½ cups of Blood Orange Whipped Cream and set aside to be used to frost the top of the cake. Using an offset spatula, spread half of the remaining Blood Orange Whipped Cream onto the syrup-soaked cake layer, allowing the whipped cream to fill up the space between the cake and the cake pan. Use a rubber spatula to gently but firmly press the whipped cream down in between the side of the cake pan and the cake layer, thus essentially forming the side of the cake. Spoon half of the raspberry–cranberry preserves mixture onto the Blood Orange Whipped Cream, gently pressing the berries onto the cream.

5. Top with a second layer of pound cake and repeat with another one-third of the simple syrup, the other half of the remaining Blood Orange Whipped Cream, and remaining raspberry–cranberry preserves mixture.

6. Top with the final layer of cake and moisten with the remaining Blood Orange Simple Syrup. Using a long, flat spatula, evenly spread the reserved 1½ cups Blood Orange Whipped Cream over the top of the cake, leaving approximately ⅛ inch of space between the top of the cake and the top edge of the cake pan to hold the Blood Orange Mirroir glaze (see Decor, step 3). Tightly wrap the cake in the pan in plastic wrap and place in the freezer overnight.

½ cup blood orange concentrate

⅓ cup granulated sugar

3 tablespoons light corn syrup

⅓ cup strained apricot preserves

3 gelatin sheets (see page 11)

1. Combine the blood orange concentrate, sugar, corn syrup, and strained preserves in a small, heavy saucepan over medium-high heat and bring to a boil, stirring constantly. Once the mixture boils, insert a candy thermometer and continue to stir continuously until the mixture reaches 230°F, about 6 minutes. Remove the saucepan from the heat.

2. While the mixture is cooking, place the gelatin sheets in 4 cups cool water for 5 minutes to soften. Squeeze out excess water from the softened gelatin and stir into the hot mixture. Return the saucepan to the heat, and cook, stirring continuously, to 240°F, about 4 minutes.

DECOR

1 recipe Blood Orange Miroir

1 ripe blood orange, thinly sliced

Fresh flowers and petals

Raspberry Sauce and Mango Sauce (page 170 or 169) (optional)

1. Remove the assembled cake from the freezer, remove the plastic wrap, and pour approximately ¾ cup of the warm Blood Orange Miroir onto the top of the frozen cake, swirling the cake pan around until the miroir completely covers the top of the entire cake. Let cool in the refrigerator for 20 to 30 minutes until set.

2. When the miroir has fully set, unmold the cake from the pan (see page 14). Using an offset spatula, smooth the outside of the cake if necessary. The top of the cake should be a glossy, dark orange, and the sides should have a very creamy, smooth, pale orange finish. Defrost the unmolded, glazed cake in the refrigerator for 8 hours or overnight.

1. When ready to serve, remove the cake from the refrigerator and place on a doily-covered, 12-inch round cake board or directly onto a cake plate. Decorate the top of the cake with fresh blood orange slices or fresh flowers. Sprinkle fresh flower petals around the base of the cake, if using. Serve slices with sauce, if desired.

Extraordinary
WINTER

Versailles

I picture Louis XIV at the height of his reign, eating this dessert in his lavish palace at Versailles. My husband, Jamie, loves caramel, and I love *nougat glacée*, a very traditional and old-fashioned French dessert studded with caramelized nuts and candied fruits. This cake modernizes that classic, and is one of two that I created for our wedding day. Caramel can be found in every layer, and caramelized nuts finish it. As an over-the-top addition, I edge the cake with caramel macarons and as the crowning touch, raspberry sauce is an absolute necessity.

ALMOND JOCONDE

MAKES ONE 8-INCH CAKE

SERVES 12

3 tablespoons unsalted butter, melted but not hot, plus 2 teaspoons, for greasing pan

2 large eggs

4 large egg yolks

⅔ cup granulated sugar

2 teaspoons honey

1 tablespoon candied orange peel, finely chopped (optional)

¾ cup almond flour

⅔ cup all-purpose flour

⅓ cup almonds, lightly toasted and cooled

4 large egg whites

1. Preheat the oven to 325°F. Grease the bottom and sides of an 8-by-3-inch round cake pan with removable bottom with 2 teaspoons of the melted butter and line the bottom with an 8-inch-diameter parchment paper round.

2. In the bowl of a stand mixer fitted with the whisk attachment, whip together the whole eggs and egg yolks with ⅓ cup of sugar on medium-high speed until light in color and thick, about 3 minutes. Add the honey and whip for another 2 minutes. The batter will continue to thicken and lighten in color. Add the chopped candied orange peel, if using, and mix until just incorporated. Remove the bowl from the mixer.

3. While the eggs are whipping, combine both flours with the almonds in the bowl of a food processor fitted with the blade attachment. Process until the mixture is ground but still has small pieces of toasted almonds in the mix. Using a rubber spatula, fold the processed mixture into the batter, being careful to not overmix. Transfer the batter to a clean mixing bowl large enough to mix in the meringue (see step 5).

4. In the bowl of a stand mixer fitted with the whisk attachment, whip the egg whites on medium speed for 2 minutes. When the egg whites are frothy, begin to slowly add the remaining ⅓ cup sugar and increase the speed to medium-high. Whip until the egg whites are stiff with a creamy texture, about 3 minutes. Remove the bowl from the mixer.

5. Using a rubber spatula, carefully fold half of the meringue and then half of the melted butter into the batter. Repeat with the remaining meringue and the remaining melted butter.

6. Pour the batter into the prepared cake pan and place on a rack in the center of the oven. Bake the cake until a knife inserted in the center comes out clean, 45 to 50 minutes. The cake will have a slightly golden color and a nutty, spongelike texture.

7. Remove the cake from the oven and allow to cool completely. Once cooled, remove the cake from the pan (see page 12) and peel the parchment paper from the bottom of the cake. Wrap the cake tightly in plastic wrap until ready to use. The Almond Joconde can be stored for up to 2 days at room temperature.

RUM SIMPLE SYRUP

(see page 68)

SALTED CARAMEL

1¾ cups heavy cream

¾ cup glucose
or light corn syrup

1 cup granulated sugar

1½ teaspoons French
sea salt (such as *sel de
Guérande*)

3 tablespoons unsalted
butter, room temperature,
cut into ¼-inch cubes

1. Bring the cream almost to a boil in a small, heavy saucepan over medium heat. Because the cream needs to be hot when incorporating it into the warm caramel, it may be necessary to hold it over very low heat once hot and until ready to use.

2. Meanwhile, combine the glucose, sugar, and salt in a medium, heavy saucepan over medium heat and boil, stirring occasionally, for approximately 15 minutes. The mixture should become light amber in color. Watch carefully, as caramel can go from light to burnt very quickly. Carefully mix in the butter and stir continuously until the thermometer reads 360°F. The caramel should continue to boil as you stir, and the color should darken to a deep golden brown.

3. Very carefully pour the warm cream into the hot caramel and stir until smooth and completely combined. *Be extremely careful when adding any liquid into a hot caramel, as the caramel may spatter.* This recipe will make about 2¼ cups of Salted Caramel. Measure out 1 cup of Salted Caramel and set it aside to be used in the Salted Caramel Mousse. Measure out ¼ cup to be used while assembling the cake. The remaining Salted Caramel, about 1 cup, will be used to decorate the cake. Store all, well wrapped in plastic wrap, in the refrigerator until ready to use. The Salted Caramel can be made up to 3 days in advance but may settle and separate. The caramel will also need to be reheated to barely hot before using (see page 12). To re-emulsify, simply stir well as the caramel is being reheated.

SALTED CARAMEL MOUSSE

2 cups heavy cream

3 tablespoons granulated
sugar

6 large egg yolks

6 gelatin sheets (see page 11)

1 cup Salted Caramel,
reheated until pourable,
not hot (see page 12)

1. In the bowl of a stand mixer fitted with the whisk attachment, whip the cream until soft peaks form, 2 minutes. Hold in the refrigerator until ready to use.

2. Combine the sugar with ¼ cup water in a small, heavy saucepan over medium heat and bring to a boil. Insert a candy thermometer and cook to 230° to 240°F, the soft-ball stage.

3. While the sugar is cooking, place the egg yolks in the bowl of a stand mixer fitted with the whisk attachment and whip at medium-high speed until thick and light, 2 to 3 minutes. Carefully pour the hot sugar syrup into the whipping yolks in a continuous stream, being careful to avoid pouring the syrup directly onto the moving whisk. Increase the mixer speed to high and whip until the mixture has cooled down and has tripled in volume, 7 to 10 minutes.

4. While the yolk mixture is whipping, soften the gelatin sheets in 6 cups cool water for 5 minutes. Squeeze out the excess water, then melt the gelatin in a small saucepan over low heat until liquid. Pour the melted gelatin into the cooled egg mixture and whip until dissolved and fully blended. Remove the bowl from the mixer.

5. Using a rubber spatula, fold in the warmed, liquid Salted Caramel. Then fold in the whipped cream until fully combined. This recipe will yield 5½ cups of mousse, all of which will be used to assemble the cake. The Salted Caramel Mousse should be made when ready to assemble the cake.

PISTACHIO ALMOND PRALINE

Grapeseed or vegetable oil for coating baking sheet

⅓ cup granulated sugar

⅓ cup sliced almonds

⅓ cup raw pistachios, shelled

1. Generously coat a baking sheet with oil or line the baking sheet with a Silpat and set aside.

2. In a medium, heavy saucepan, bring the sugar and 2 tablespoons water to a boil over medium-high heat. Using a heat-resistant rubber spatula, stir in the almonds and pistachios. Mix continuously until the cooked sugar coats the nuts in a sandlike consistency. Continue to mix and cook until the nuts become glossy and take on a caramelized color, about 3 minutes.

3. Using an offset spatula, carefully spread the hot nut mixture onto the prepared baking sheet and set aside to cool. The Pistachio Almond Praline can be made 1 to 2 days in advance and stored in an airtight container to avoid becoming moist and sticky, but is best when made on the day it is being used.

ASSEMBLY

Almond Joconde, baked and cooled

1 recipe Rum Simple Syrup

1 recipe Salted Caramel Mousse

¼ cup Salted Caramel, reheated as necessary (see page 12)

1. Place the unwrapped joconde on a clean, flat work surface. Using a long serrated knife, slice off the very top of the cake to even out as necessary— approximately ⅛ inch. Slice the cake horizontally into 3 even layers.

2. Using an 8-inch round cake board as the bottom of an 8-by-3-inch round cake pan with removable bottom (see page 13), place 1 cake layer on the cake board, cut side up. Using a pastry brush, moisten the cake layer with one-third of the Rum Simple Syrup.

3. Using an offset spatula, spread 2¼ cups of Salted Caramel Mousse, evenly onto the syrup-soaked cake layer and drizzle with 2 tablespoons of Salted Caramel.

4. Top with a second layer of cake and repeat with another one-third of the simple syrup, 2¼ cups of Salted Caramel Mousse, and 2 tablespoons of Salted Caramel.

5. Top with the final layer of cake, moisten with the remaining Rum Simple Syrup, and cover with remaining Salted Caramel Mousse (about 1 cup). Use a long metal spatula to evenly spread the mousse so that the top of the cake is nice and flat. Tightly wrap the cake in the pan in plastic wrap and place in the freezer overnight.

2 gelatin sheets (see page 11)

1 cup Salted Caramel

Pistachio Almond Praline, finely ground in a food processor

6 to 7 purchased caramel macarons (see page 171) (optional)

1 yard of satin ribbon

1 floral pin

Fresh flowers or flower petals

Raspberry Sauce and Vanilla Sauce, or Caramel Sauce (page 170 or 168) (optional)

1. Soften the gelatin sheets in 2 cups cool water for 5 minutes. Squeeze out the excess water, then melt the gelatin in a small saucepan over low heat until liquid.

2. Gently reheat the salted caramel in a small, heavy saucepan over low heat until pourable but not hot, stirring to re-emulsify as needed. Remove from the heat and whisk in the liquefied gelatin until fully combined.

3. Remove the assembled cake from the freezer, remove the plastic wrap, and unmold the cake from the pan (see page 14). Place the cake on a wire rack set over a baking sheet. Pour half of the warm caramel over the top and sides of the cake and return the cake to the freezer for 15 minutes to firm up. Repeat this one more time with the remaining caramel, until the top and sides of the cake have a very finished look. If the caramel cools down and begins to thicken before coating the cake a second time, it may need to be gently reheated over low heat. After the second coat, place the caramel-covered cake back in the freezer for an additional 15 minutes to set.

4. Remove the caramel-covered cake from the freezer and edge the sides with the ground Pistachio Almond Praline. Place the cake on a doily-covered, 10-inch round cake board or directly onto a cake plate. Separate the macarons and gently press the macaron halves around the base of the cake.

5. Measure the ribbon so that it is long enough to fit around the cake with plenty of ribbon to create a bow (it is like tying a shoelace). The ribbon can be centered halfway up the cake or around the bottom, according to your preference. An option is to create a bow and tie it in the center or simply wrap the ribbon around the cake and pin it in place without a bow.

6. Return the decorated cake to the refrigerator for 4 to 6 hours to fully defrost. Allow the cake to come to room temperature for 1 hour before serving. Top the center of the cake with fresh flowers or fresh flower petals. Serve slices with sauce, if desired.

Holiday Yule Log

Around the world, holidays are a time for family and tradition. In my family, the holidays also call for good food, and it always falls to me to provide delicious, decadent desserts. This recipe is traditional yet spectacular, and could serve quite well as the centerpiece for any holiday table.

The cake layer combines characteristics of both brownies and chocolate soufflés. In addition, bits of cherries soaked in raspberry tea impart a bold, fruity taste. Because the Yule Log is so moist and dense, it requires a long time to bake, so plan accordingly. Serve freshly whipped cream, vanilla ice cream, or vanilla sauce alongside to highlight the sublime chocolate texture.

BITTERSWEET CHOCOLATE BROWNIE CAKE

MAKES 1 LOG-SHAPED CAKE

SERVES 12 TO 14

1 cup unsalted butter,
room temperature,
cut into ¼-inch cubes,
plus 2 teaspoons, melted
but not hot, for greasing pan

1 tablespoon loose-leaf
raspberry tea

1 cup dried tart cherries,
diced

½ cup all-purpose flour

2 cups raw almonds

14 ounces (2½ cups)
72% bittersweet chocolate,
coarsely chopped

6 large eggs, separated

1¼ cups plus ⅓ cup
granulated sugar

2 teaspoons vanilla extract

1. Preheat the oven to 300°F. Grease the bottom and sides of a 12-by-3½-by-4-inch rectangular cake pan with the 2 teaspoons melted butter.

2. Bring 1 cup water to a boil and add the raspberry tea. Steep the tea for 3 minutes, then strain into a clean mixing bowl. Add the cherries and soak for 1 hour. Drain the tea-soaked cherries and set aside, discarding the soaking liquid.

3. Sift the flour into the bowl of a food processor fitted with the blade attachment, add the almonds, and process until the mixture is finely ground.

4. Melt the chocolate with ¼ cup water in a small, heavy saucepan over low heat, stirring occasionally. When the chocolate and water are melted and smooth, add the cubed butter one piece at a time, stirring continuously over low heat until the mixture is smooth and homogenous.

5. In the bowl of a stand mixer fitted with the whisk attachment, whip the 6 egg yolks with 1¼ cups sugar until thickened in volume and light in color, about 5 minutes. With the mixer running, add the vanilla and the melted chocolate mixture to the egg yolks, whisking until smooth. Remove the bowl from the mixer. Using a rubber spatula, fold first the freshly processed mixture and then the cherries into the batter, being careful not to overmix. Transfer the batter to a clean mixing bowl large enough to mix in the meringue (see step 7).

6. In the bowl of a stand mixer fitted with the whisk attachment, whip the egg whites on medium speed for 2 minutes. When the egg whites are frothy, begin to slowly add ⅓ cup sugar and increase the mixer speed to medium-high. Whip until the egg whites are stiff with a creamy texture, about 5 minutes. Remove the bowl from the mixer.

7. Using a rubber spatula, carefully fold the meringue into the chocolate cake batter in several additions, until well incorporated.

8. Pour the batter into the prepared cake pan. Cover the pan with aluminum foil, poke 2 holes in the top of the foil, and place on a rack in the center of the oven. Bake for 90 minutes. Uncover the cake and bake for another 15 minutes. The cake is done when you can touch the cake and your finger comes away clean. The baked cake should be firm but spongy and the edges should pull away from the sides of the pan. Inserting a knife is not a way to test for doneness, because this cake will be very moist even when it is ready to take out of the oven.

9. Remove the cake from the oven and allow the cake to cool completely in the pan. Once cooled, tightly wrap the cake in the pan in plastic wrap and place in the freezer for 2 hours or overnight. The Bittersweet Chocolate Brownie Cake can be stored for 1 to 2 weeks in the freezer.

SEMISWEET CHOCOLATE RASPBERRY TEA GANACHE

18 ounces (3 cups)
semisweet chocolate chips

1½ cups heavy cream

1 tablespoon loose-leaf
raspberry tea

1. Place the chocolate chips in a medium, heatproof mixing bowl.

2. Bring the cream to a boil in a small, heavy saucepan over medium-high heat. Remove from the heat, add the tea, and steep for 3 minutes. Straining through a fine-mesh sieve, pour the hot cream over the chocolate and let sit for 5 minutes. Using a rubber spatula, stir slowly and gently in a circular motion until the mixture is fully combined and homogenous.

3. Transfer the chocolate mixture to a food processor and process to blend (or, using an immersion blender, blend to emulsify). The ganache should be thick and shiny. It is preferable to make the Semisweet Chocolate Raspberry Tea Ganache when you are ready to use it. This recipe will yield 2¾ cups of ganache. Two cups will be used to cover the cake and ¾ cup will be used to make the rosettes (see Decor).

ASSEMBLY

Bittersweet Chocolate
Brownie Cake

¼ cup raspberry or cherry
preserves, strained

2 cups Semisweet
Chocolate Raspberry
Tea Ganache

1. Remove the cake from the freezer, remove the plastic wrap, and unmold the cake from the pan (see page 14). Place the cake on a clean rectangular cake board cut to size. Allow the cake to thaw at room temperature for 3 to 4 hours before frosting.

2. Using an offset spatula, spread the preserves evenly over the top of the cake. Cover the cake with the Semisweet Chocolate Raspberry Tea Ganache, spreading it evenly over the top and sides. Place the frosted cake, unwrapped, in the freezer for 15 minutes to allow the ganache to fully set.

DARK CHOCOLATE GLAZE

6 ounces (1 cup) 56% to 60%
dark chocolate, coarsely chopped

3 tablespoons grapeseed
or vegetable oil

2 tablespoons granulated sugar

⅓ cup heavy cream

1 tablespoon glucose
or light corn syrup

1. Place the chocolate in a medium, microwave-safe mixing bowl and microwave in 30-second intervals until melted, stirring each time between intervals. Pour the oil into the melted chocolate and mix until smooth and homogenous.

2. While the chocolate is melting, combine the sugar and 2 tablespoons water in a small, heavy saucepan over medium-high heat and bring to a boil, stirring occasionally. Remove from the heat and mix in the cream and glucose. Return to the heat and bring to a boil.

3. Slowly whisk the hot mixture into the melted warm chocolate a little bit at a time. Whisk until smooth and glossy. Strain through a medium-mesh sieve into a clean bowl. The Dark Chocolate Glaze is best made when ready to glaze the cake.

BITTERSWEET CHOCOLATE ALMOND TUILE

2 teaspoons grapeseed
or vegetable oil

½ cup unsalted butter,
room temperature,
cut into ¼-inch cubes

¼ cup whole milk

2 tablespoons glucose
or light corn syrup

½ cup granulated sugar

1 teaspoon pectin (optional)

¼ cup cocoa powder, sifted

1 cup sliced almonds

1. Generously coat a baking sheet with the oil, or use a silicone liner.

2. Melt together the butter, milk, glucose, sugar, and, if using, the pectin in a medium, heavy saucepan over medium heat. Bring to a boil and stir continuously until thickened and glossy, about 10 minutes. If using a candy thermometer, cook to 330°F. Remove the saucepan from the heat and whisk in the cocoa powder. When the cocoa is fully dissolved, stir in the almonds.

3. Using an offset spatula, spread the batter thinly onto the prepared baking sheet.

4. Let cool to room temperature. The tuile will be the color of dark chocolate and very crispy. The Bittersweet Chocolate Almond Tuile should be made the same day that you are using it, or it will become sticky and moist.

1 recipe Dark Chocolate Glaze, warm

¾ cup Semisweet Chocolate Raspberry Tea Ganache

1 recipe Bittersweet Chocolate Almond Tuile

Fresh strawberries, raspberries, and red currants to taste

Dark chocolate shavings (see page 16)

Whipped cream (optional)

Vanilla Sauce and/or Chocolate Sauce (page 170 and 169) (optional)

1. Remove the ganache-covered cake from the freezer and place on a wire rack set over a baking sheet. Generously pour the warm Dark Chocolate Glaze over the cake, making sure to completely cover the top and sides for a smooth, even appearance. Place the cake in the refrigerator for 15 minutes to set.

2. Fit a pastry bag with a ½-inch, 8-point, open star decorating tip and fill with the Semisweet Chocolate Raspberry Tea Ganache. Pipe rosettes down the center of the cake. Place the decorated cake on a serving platter.

3. Break up the cooled Bittersweet Chocolate Almond Tuile into large, fan-shaped pieces. Stick different sized pieces of chocolate tuile into each of the rosettes, creating an abstract, fanlike appearance down the center of the Holiday Yule Log. The tuile pieces should all be different shapes and sizes and should point asymmetrically all over the top of the yule log.

4. Crumble up any remaining chocolate tuile and place crumbs around the bottom 1½-inch border of the cake. Cluster together fresh berries and red currants on the top of the yule log in between the chocolate tuiles. Top with chocolate shavings.

5. Allow the Holiday Yule Log to come to room temperature for 3 hours before serving. Serve slices with whipped cream or sauce, if desired.

Raspberry White Chocolate Linzer Torte

Rich, nutty, moist, and bursting with raspberries, this is a spin on the famous linzertortes of Austria, Switzerland, and Hungary. The sweet White Chocolate Buttercream perfectly complements the other flavors, and when allowed to rest at room temperature for 2 hours, this extravagant creation becomes even more irresistible. My Linzer Torte can even serve as a fabulous wedding cake.

Keep this tip in mind if preparing dacquoise for the first time: Avoid overbeating the meringue, or it will deflate when folded into the nuts.

HAZELNUT ALMOND CAKE

MAKES ONE 10-INCH
SQUARE CAKE

SERVES 20 TO 24

2 teaspoons unsalted
butter, melted but not hot

½ cup skinned hazelnut
pieces, toasted and cooled
(see page 12)

¼ cup sliced almonds,
skins on, toasted and
cooled (see page 12)

3 cups all-purpose flour,
sifted

1 teaspoon baking powder

2⅔ cups heavy cream

½ teaspoon almond extract

1 teaspoon vanilla extract

6 large eggs

1¾ cups granulated sugar

1. Preheat the oven to 300°F. Grease the bottom and sides of a 10-by-3-inch square cake pan with removable bottom with the melted butter and line the bottom with a 10-inch square piece of parchment paper.

2. In the bowl of a food processor fitted with the blade attachment, coarsely grind the nuts in several batches, taking care not to overprocess and release the oil from the nuts.

3. Sift together the flour and baking powder into a clean bowl. Add the ground nuts and mix together. Transfer to a food processor fitted with the blade attachment and pulse to a semi-fine powder.

4. In the bowl of a stand mixer fitted with the whisk attachment, whip together the cream with the almond and vanilla extracts for 1 to 2 minutes, until thick but not whipped enough to hold its shape. Set at room temperature.

5. In the bowl of a stand mixer fitted with the whisk attachment, whip together the eggs and sugar at medium-high speed until light in color and thick, about 10 minutes. Using a rubber spatula, scrape down the sides of the bowl, then whip for an additional 2 minutes. Remove the bowl from the mixer. Using a rubber spatula, fold the barely whipped cream into the egg mixture until combined. Next, gently fold the processed ingredients into the batter until smooth.

6. Pour the batter into the prepared cake pan and place on a rack in the center of the oven. Bake until golden brown, about 85 minutes. The top of the cake may crack while baking and it will begin to lightly brown all over.

7. Remove the cake from the oven and allow to cool. Once cooled, remove the cake from the pan (see page 12) and peel the parchment paper from the bottom of the cake. Wrap the cake tightly in plastic wrap until ready to use. The Hazelnut Almond Cake can be stored for up to 2 days at room temperature.

RUM SIMPLE SYRUP

½ cup granulated sugar

¼ cup Myer's dark rum

1. Combine the sugar with ½ cup water in a small, heavy saucepan over medium-high heat and bring to a boil, stirring occasionally. Remove from the heat, pour into a clean bowl, and allow to cool.

2. Once fully cooled, stir in the rum until combined. The Rum Simple Syrup will keep for up to 3 days in an airtight container in the refrigerator.

WHITE CHOCOLATE GANACHE

8 ounces (1¼ cups) good-quality white chocolate, coarsely chopped

1 cup heavy cream

1. Place the white chocolate in a small, heatproof mixing bowl.

2. Bring the cream to a boil in a small, heavy saucepan over medium-high heat. Pour the hot cream over the white chocolate and let sit for a couple of minutes before whisking until smooth and fully combined.

3. Allow the ganache to cool to the consistency of loose pudding. The White Chocolate Ganache can be made up to 5 days in advance and kept in an airtight container in the refrigerator, but may need to be gently reheated before using (see page 12).

ITALIAN MERINGUE

2 large egg whites (reserve the yolks for use in the White Chocolate Buttercream)

Scant ⅔ cup granulated sugar

1. In the bowl of a stand mixer fitted with the whisk attachment, whip the egg whites on medium speed for 2 minutes. When the egg whites are frothy, slowly add 3 tablespoons of sugar and increase the speed to medium-high. Whip until the egg whites are stiff with a creamy texture, about 3 minutes. If you reach a stiff meringue before the sugar has fully cooked (see step 2), reduce the mixer speed to low until the hot sugar syrup is ready.

2. While the whites are whipping, combine the remaining sugar with 3 table-spoons water in a small, heavy saucepan and bring to a boil. Insert a candy thermometer and cook to 230° to 240°F, the soft-ball stage.

3. With the mixer on medium-high speed, carefully pour the hot sugar syrup into the whipping meringue in a continuous stream, being careful to avoid pouring the syrup directly onto the moving whisk. Increase the mixer speed to high and whisk until the meringue has cooled down, about 4 minutes. Once cooled, the meringue should have a thick and gooey consistency. Transfer the Italian Meringue to a clean container and cover with plastic wrap. Store in the refrigerator if using the same day. It may also be stored in an airtight container in the freezer for up to 5 days if making in advance. The Italian Meringue can be used frozen.

½ cup whole milk

½ teaspoon vanilla extract

Scant ¾ cup granulated sugar

8 large egg yolks

4⅓ cups unsalted butter, room temperature, cut into ¼-inch cubes

1 recipe Italian Meringue

1 recipe White Chocolate Ganache, room temperature (see page 12)

1. In a medium, heavy saucepan over medium-high heat, bring the milk, vanilla, and 6 tablespoons of sugar to a boil.

2. Meanwhile, whisk together the remaining 10 tablespoons sugar and the egg yolks in a heatproof, nonreactive mixing bowl until well combined and smooth. While whisking continuously, slowly pour the warm milk mixture into the egg mixture and whisk until well incorporated. Return the milk-egg mixture to the saucepan, insert a candy thermometer, and cook over medium heat, stirring gently with a rubber spatula, until the mixture begins to thicken and has reached 150°F, 3 to 4 minutes.

3. Strain the mixture through a fine-mesh sieve into the clean bowl of a stand mixer fitted with the whisk attachment. Whip on medium-high speed until cooled, thickened, and pale yellow in color, about 6 minutes. Reduce the mixer speed to low and add the butter, ½ cup at a time, until fully incorporated. Add the Italian Meringue, increasing the mixer speed as necessary to fully incorporate. Once fully combined, remove the bowl from the mixer.

4. Using a whisk, mix in the White Chocolate Ganache until smooth and fully combined. Measure out 2½ cups of the White Chocolate Buttercream and set aside to be used for the final Decor. Cover all with plastic wrap and refrigerate until ready to use. The White Chocolate Buttercream can be made up to 3 days in advance. Allow the White Chocolate Buttercream to come to room temperature before using, or reheat in a microwave in multiple 20-second intervals, whisking vigorously by hand after each interval, to obtain the buttercream's original texture.

1 teaspoon unsalted butter, melted but not hot

½ cup skinned hazelnuts, toasted and cooled

½ cup sliced almonds, skins on, toasted and cooled

1 teaspoon arrowroot or cornstarch

4 large egg whites (reserve the yolks for use in the White Chocolate Buttercream)

⅓ cup granulated sugar

1. Preheat the oven to 250°F. Using a pencil, trace a 10-inch square onto a sheet of parchment paper. Flip the paper, pencil side down, onto a baking sheet and lightly brush the square with the melted butter.

2. In the bowl of a food processor fitted with the blade attachment, finely grind both nuts with the arrowroot.

3. In the bowl of a stand mixer fitted with the whisk attachment, whip the egg whites on medium speed for 2 minutes. When the egg whites are frothy, begin to slowly add the sugar and increase the speed to medium-high. Whip until the egg whites are stiff with a creamy texture, about 4 minutes. Remove the bowl from the mixer.

4. Using a rubber spatula, carefully fold the nut mixture into the meringue until combined. Fit a pastry bag with a ½-inch plain round decorating tip and fill with the dacquoise batter. Starting in the center of the traced square on the sheet of parchment paper and working in a counter-clockwise direction, pipe the batter in a square spiral to completely fill in the outline.

5. Place the piped dacquoise on the baking sheet on a rack in the center of the oven and bake until the dacquoise is crisp, slightly browned, and dry to the touch, about 65 minutes. The Hazelnut Almond Dacquoise can be made up to 1 day in advance and stored uncovered in a cool, dry oven.

ASSEMBLY

⅔ cup (from one 8-ounce jar) raspberry preserves (with seeds)

2 pints fresh raspberries

Hazelnut Almond Cake, baked and cooled

1 recipe Rum Simple Syrup

7 cups White Chocolate Buttercream, room temperature (see page 12)

Hazelnut Almond Dacquoise, baked and cooled

1. Combine the raspberry preserves with the fresh raspberries and set aside.

2. Place the unwrapped cake on a clean, flat work surface. Using a long serrated knife, slice off the top ¼ inch to even out the top of the cake as necessary. Slice the cake horizontally into 2 even ½- to ⅝-inch-thick layers.

3. Using a 10-inch square cake board as the bottom of a sqaure 10-by-3-inch cake pan with removable bottom (see page 13), place 1 cake layer on the cake board, cut side up. Using a pastry brush, moisten the cake layer with half of the Rum Simple Syrup.

4. Using an offset spatula, spread 2½ cups White Chocolate Buttercream evenly onto the syrup-soaked cake layer and top with half of the raspberry preserves mixture. Cover with the Hazelnut Almond Dacquoise, piped side down so that it is flat on top, and press firmly in place. Repeat with 2 cups buttercream and the remaining raspberry mixture.

5. Top with a second cake layer and moisten with the remaining Rum Simple Syrup. Using a long metal spatula, cover with the remaining 2½ cups White Chocolate Buttercream, spreading it very evenly over the cake. It is important to spread this layer as smoothly as possible, as this will be the top of the cake. Place the cake in the freezer, unwrapped to avoid any marks, until the buttercream is very firm. Then tightly wrap the cake in the pan in plastic wrap and place in the freezer overnight or for up to 1 week.

DECOR

Reserved 2½ cups White Chocolate Buttercream, room temperature (see page 12)

3½ feet of gold cording, approximately ½ inch thick (or your choice of ribbon)

1 pearlhead pin

3 sheets edible gold leaf (see page 16)

Fresh flowers

Raspberry Sauce (page 170) (optional)

1. Remove the assembled cake from the freezer, remove the plastic wrap, and release the cake from the pan (see page 14). Using a long, flat spatula, cover the sides and smooth over the top of the cake with the reserved White Chocolate Buttercream, spreading as evenly as possible. To create a very smooth and finished cake surface, after applying all of the buttercream, dip the spatula in hot water and run it around the sides and across the top of the cake.

2. Place the frosted cake on a serving platter and wrap the cording around the base of the cake, securing with the pin. Transfer the decorated cake to the refrigerator for 8 to 10 hours or overnight to fully defrost.

3. Finish with fresh flowers edged with gold leaf and allow the cake to sit at room temperature for 2 hours before serving. Serve slices with sauce, if desired.

Amor Chocolat

Port is a fortified wine generally served at the end of a meal. Any wine considered genuine port must be made from grapes grown in the Douro region of Portugal, and bottled there, too. Ports range in style and flavor, are mostly full-bodied, and pair exceptionally well with chocolate.

On a recent trip, my family fell so in love with the Douro region that I decided to create a cake to marry these flavors. With layers of both milk and dark chocolate accented by port, Amor Chocolat does exactly this. I used a ruby port because it complements various types of chocolate, but a Late Bottled Vintage (LBV) also would work well.

CHOCOLATE SOUR CREAM CAKE

MAKES ONE 10-INCH CAKE

SERVES 18 TO 20

⅓ cup unsalted butter,
room temperature,
cut into ¼-inch cubes,
plus 2 teaspoons, melted but
not hot, for greasing pan

3 ounces (½ cup)
unsweetened chocolate,
coarsely chopped

1½ cups all-purpose flour

2 teaspoons baking soda

1 teaspoon baking powder

2 large eggs

1½ cups granulated sugar

½ cup sour cream, room
temperature

1. Preheat the oven to 275°F. Grease the bottom and sides of a 10-by-3-inch round cake pan with removable bottom with the 2 teaspoons melted butter and line the bottom with a 10-inch parchment paper round.

2. Melt the chocolate in a heatproof mixing bowl set over a pan of simmering water (do not allow the bowl to touch the water), stirring occasionally.

3. In a small mixing bowl, stir together the flour, baking soda, and baking powder until thoroughly blended. Set aside.

4. In the bowl of a stand mixer fitted with the whisk attachment, whip the eggs and sugar at medium-high speed until the mixture becomes very thick and lightens in color, about 7 minutes. Add the cubed butter and then the sour cream, mixing until fully incorporated each time, scraping down the sides of the bowl as needed. Pour in the melted, warm chocolate and continue to mix until fully incorporated. Scrape down the sides of the bowl and add the sifted ingredients, being careful not to overmix the batter.

5. In a separate small, heavy saucepan, bring 1 cup water to a boil and pour it into the batter. Mix just until fully combined and smooth. The batter will thin out considerably with the addition of the water.

6. Pour the batter into the prepared cake pan and place on a rack in the center of the oven. Bake until the cake springs back slightly when pressed and the blade of an inserted knife or cake tester comes out clean, about 60 minutes.

7. Remove the cake from the oven and allow to cool completely. Once cooled, unmold the cake from the pan (see page 12) and peel the parchment paper from the bottom of the cake. Wrap the cake tightly in plastic until ready to use. The Chocolate Sour Cream Cake can be stored for up to 2 days at room temperature.

PORT REDUCTION

3 cups good-quality ruby
red port

Heat the port in a small, heavy saucepan over medium heat until syrupy and reduced to approximately ⅔ cup, about 15 minutes. Pour the reduction into a clean bowl and allow to cool. The Port Reduction will keep for up to 3 days in an airtight container in the refrigerator.

PORT SIMPLE SYRUP

½ cup granulated sugar

⅓ cup Port Reduction

1. Combine the sugar with ⅓ cup water in a small, heavy saucepan over medium-high heat and bring to a boil, stirring occasionally. Remove from the heat, pour into a clean bowl, and allow to cool.

2. Once fully cooled, stir in the Port Reduction until combined. The Port Simple Syrup will keep for up to 3 days in an airtight container in the refrigerator.

SEMISWEET CHOCOLATE PORT GANACHE

12 ounces (2 cups)
semisweet chocolate chips

1 cup heavy cream

⅓ cup Port Reduction

1. Place the chocolate chips in a medium, heatproof mixing bowl.

2. Bring the cream to a boil in a small, heavy saucepan over medium-high heat. Pour the hot cream over the chocolate chips and let sit for 5 minutes. Using a rubber spatula, stir slowly and gently in a circular motion until the mixture is fully combined and homogenous.

3. Transfer the chocolate mixture to a food processor; add the Port Reduction and process to blend (or, using an immersion blender, add the Port Reduction to the bowl with the chocolate and cream and blend to emulsify). The ganache should be thick and shiny.

4. Pour the ganache into a clean bowl and allow to cool and firm to the consistency of pudding. The Semisweet Chocolate Port Ganache can be made up to 3 days in advance and kept in an airtight container in the refrigerator but may need to be gently reheated before using (see page 12).

MILK CHOCOLATE CRÈME BRÛLÉE

5 ounces (¾ cup) 40% milk chocolate, finely chopped

2 ounces (⅓ cup) 55% semisweet chocolate, finely chopped

8 large egg yolks

¼ cup plus 2 tablespoons granulated sugar

3 cups heavy cream

1 whole vanilla bean, scraped (see page 12)

1. Preheat the oven to 250°F.

2. Melt both of the chocolates in a medium, heatproof mixing bowl set over a pan of simmering water (do not allow the bowl to touch the water), stirring occasionally. Once melted, remove the bowl from over the water and set aside.

3. In a separate heatproof, nonreactive mixing bowl, whisk together the egg yolks and sugar until frothy.

4. Bring the cream and vanilla bean seeds to a boil in a medium, heavy saucepan over medium-high heat. While whisking continuously, slowly pour the warm cream over the egg mixture and whisk until well blended. Strain through a fine-mesh sieve into the warm, melted chocolate and stir gently to combine.

5. Pour the mixture into a 10-by-3-inch round cake pan (not a pan with a removable bottom) and bake for 30 minutes, or until set. The crème brûlée may crack, and the center of the baked crème brûlée will still jiggle slightly when set.

6. When baked, remove the crème brûlée from the oven and allow to cool to room temperature. Before unmolding from the pan, wrap the crème brûlée tightly in plastic wrap and freeze for 4 to 6 hours, until firm. The Milk Chocolate Crème Brûlée can be made up to 3 days in advance and stored in the freezer.

BITTERSWEET CHOCOLATE MOUSSE

8 ounces (1⅓ cups) 64% bittersweet chocolate, coarsely chopped

½ cup unsalted butter, room temperature, cut into ¼-inch cubes

6 large eggs, separated

6 tablespoons granulated sugar

1. Melt together the chopped chocolate and butter in a heatproof mixing bowl set over a saucepan of simmering water (do not allow the bowl to touch the water), stirring occasionally. Once melted, remove the bowl from over the water and set aside.

2. In the bowl of a stand mixer fitted with the whisk attachment, whip the egg yolks and 3 tablespoons of the sugar on medium-high speed until pale yellow in color and thick, about 5 minutes. Add the melted chocolate mixture to the yolk mixture and continue mixing for another 2 minutes. Remove the bowl from the mixer. Transfer the batter to a clean mixing bowl large enough to mix in the meringue (see step 4).

3. In the clean bowl of a stand mixer fitted with the whisk attachment, whip the egg whites on medium speed for 2 minutes. When the egg whites are frothy, begin to slowly add the remaining 3 tablespoons sugar and increase the mixer speed to medium-high. Whip until the egg whites are stiff with a creamy texture, about 5 minutes. Remove the bowl from the mixer.

4. Using a rubber spatula, fold the meringue into the batter just until the mousse is evenly mixed throughout. The Bittersweet Chocolate Mousse should be made when ready to assemble the cake.

Milk Chocolate Crème Brûlée

Chocolate Sour Cream Cake, baked and cooled

1 recipe Port Simple Syrup

1 recipe Semisweet Chocolate Port Ganache

1 recipe Bittersweet Chocolate Mousse

1. Remove the Milk Chocolate Crème Brûlée from the freezer, remove the plastic wrap, and unmold by first running a hot knife around the inside of the cake pan. Next, using a hair dryer set on low, gently heat the bottom of the pan to release the crème brûlée (hold the pan in one hand and rotate the pan while you heat it from underneath and around the sides with the hair dryer). Flip the loosened crème brûlée onto a 10-inch round card-board cake board. Keep the crème brûlée in the freezer until ready to use.

2. Place the unwrapped cake on a flat work surface. Using a long serrated knife, slice off the top ¼ inch of the cake to even out the top of the cake as necessary. Slice the cake horizontally into three ¼-inch-thick layers.

3. Using a 10-inch round cake board as the bottom of a 10-by-3-inch round cake pan with removable bottom (see page 13), place 1 cake layer on the cake board, cut side up. Using a pastry brush, moisten the cake layer with one-third of the Port Simple Syrup.

4. Using an offset spatula, spread approximately ¾ cup of cooled Semisweet Chocolate Port Ganache evenly over the cake and top with the frozen Milk Chocolate Crème Brûlée.

5. Top with a second layer of cake and repeat with another one-third of the simple syrup and another ¾ cup of ganache. Using an offset spatula, spread all of the Bittersweet Chocolate Mousse evenly over the ganache.

6. Top with the final layer of cake, moisten with the remaining Port Simple Syrup, and cover with remaining Semisweet Chocolate Port Ganache. Tightly wrap the cake in the pan in plastic wrap and place in the freezer overnight.

CHOCOLATE SHORTBREAD

¼ cup plus 1 tablespoon unsalted butter, room temperature, cut into ¼-inch cubes, plus 2 teaspoons, melted but not hot, for greasing baking sheet

¼ cup turbinado sugar

2 tablespoons granulated sugar

2 teaspoons vanilla extract

2 tablespoons cocoa powder

¼ teaspoon baking soda

½ cup all-purpose flour

¼ teaspoon French sea salt (such as *sel de Guérande*)

1. Preheat the oven to 300°F. Grease a baking sheet with the 2 teaspoons melted butter or line with a Silpat and set aside.

2. Combine the cubed butter and both sugars in a medium mixing bowl. Using your hands, work the butter and sugars together. Work in the vanilla extract until a sandy texture is achieved.

3. Sift together the cocoa powder, baking soda, and flour and with your hands work them into the butter-sugar mixture to create a soft dough.

4. Using your hands, crumble the dough into small pieces all over the prepared baking sheet. Place the baking sheet on a rack in the center of the oven and bake until the shortbread is crisp, about 20 minutes.

5. Remove the shortbread from the oven and allow to cool completely. If the shortbread crumbles spread together during baking, simply chop them up coarsely when ready. The Chocolate Shortbread is best made the day you plan to decorate the cake.

DARK CHOCOLATE MIROIR

¼ cup granulated sugar

2 tablespoons cocoa powder, sifted

2 tablespoons heavy cream

1 gelatin sheet (see page 11)

1 tablespoon glucose
or light corn syrup

1. Combine the sugar, cocoa powder, and heavy cream with 2 tablespoons water in a small, heavy saucepan over medium-high heat and bring to a boil. Remove the pan from the heat.

2. While the sugar is cooking, place the gelatin sheet in 2 cups cool water for 3 minutes to soften. Squeeze out excess water from the gelatin and add to the hot sugar mixture along with the glucose. Mix well to combine.

3. I prefer to use the Dark Chocolate Miroir immediately after making it. However, it can be made up to 3 days in advance and stored in an airtight container in the refrigerator, but will need to be reheated until warm and liquid before using.

DECOR

1 recipe Dark Chocolate Miroir, warm

1 recipe Chocolate Shortbread, chopped

3 to 6 fresh red roses

Chocolate Sauce or Vanilla Sauce (page 169 or 170) (optional)

1. Remove the assembled cake from the freezer, remove the plastic wrap, and unmold the cake from the pan (see page 14). Place the cake on a wire rack set over a baking sheet. Pour the warm Dark Chocolate Miroir onto the frozen cake, using a long metal spatula to spread it evenly over the top and down the sides of the cake. The miroir is very glossy and you want to work with it quickly; a thin layer is all that is necessary to leave a very clean finish. Place the cake in the refrigerator for 20 minutes to allow the miroir to fully set.

2. Remove the cake from the refrigerator and press the chopped Chocolate Shortbread evenly around the sides of the cake to cover the glaze. Pull some of the roses apart into petals. Decorate the top of the cake with whole roses and petals as desired.

1. Allow the decorated cake to fully defrost in the refrigerator for 6 hours. Remove from the refrigerator up to 1 hour before serving and let sit at room temperature to bring out the full flavor of the port. Serve slices with sauce, if desired.

Love Is Chocolate

This chocolate bread pudding is not only one of the most popular desserts in my repertoire, but also one of the simplest to make. Essentially a spin on the French breakfast pastry, *pain au chocolat,* my version is buttery and crunchy, and best of all, gushing with chocolate! Delicious either on a brunch buffet or as dessert, to enjoy this cake at its best, be sure to serve it warm.

VANILLA CRÈME BRÛLÉE MIXTURE

MAKES ONE 10-INCH BREAD PUDDING

SERVES 10 TO 12

13 large egg yolks

1 cup plus 1 tablespoon granulated sugar

4 cups heavy cream

½ cup whole milk

1 whole vanilla bean, scraped (see page 12)

1. In a heatproof, nonreactive mixing bowl, whisk together the egg yolks and sugar.

2. Bring the cream, milk, and vanilla bean seeds to a boil in a medium, heavy saucepan over medium-high heat. While whisking continuously, slowly pour the warm cream over the egg mixture and whisk until well blended.

3. Strain through a fine-mesh sieve into a clean bowl and set aside. The Vanilla Crème Brûlée Mixture may be made up to 2 days in advance if kept in an airtight container in the refrigerator. The Vanilla Crème Brûlée Mixture can be used cold or at room temperature.

ASSEMBLY

8 to 9 medium-to-large (about 3 ounces each) bakery-quality purchased all-butter croissants

1 recipe Vanilla Crème Brûlée Mixture

12 ounces (2 cups) 64% bittersweet chocolate, coarsely chopped

1. Preheat the oven to 250°F. Remove the bottom of a 10-by-4-inch springform angel food cake pan and cover with a large square of aluminum foil. Click the bottom of the pan back in place so that the excess aluminum foil sticks out the sides. Fold the excess foil up and around the outside of the pan to form a collar. This will prevent the Vanilla Crème Brûlée Mixture from leaking out of the bottom of the pan as it bakes. Place the foil-lined cake pan on a baking sheet.

2. Using a serrated knife, cut 3 of the croissants into 1-inch square pieces and set aside. Repeat with the remaining 5 to 6 croissants and keep them separated for the second layer.

3. Pour 1½ cups of the Vanilla Crème Brulée Mixture into the bottom of the prepared cake pan. Layer the first batch of croissant pieces on top of the batter in the pan. Push the croissant pieces down slightly to submerge them in the liquid, to completely cover the bottom of the pan. Spread the chopped chocolate evenly over the croissant pieces. Spoon 1 cup of Crème Brûlée Mixture over the chocolate, and pile all the remaining croissant pieces on top, leaving

approximately 1 inch between the croissant layer and the top of the pan. Depending on the size of the croissants, you may have pieces leftover. These can be stored in the freezer for the next time you make this dessert.

4. Pour the remaining Vanilla Crème Brûlée Mixture slowly and carefully over the croissants. The croissant will soak up a lot of liquid, so you may want to pour the batter in gradually and slowly to make sure that it is being soaked up. Be sure to use all of the batter so that your bread pudding will be very moist and rich after baking.

5. Place the bread pudding on the baking sheet on a rack in the center of the oven and bake for 90 minutes. The top will be crusty and toasted and the Vanilla Crème Brûlée Mixture will have firmed up into a baked custard.

6. Remove the bread pudding from the oven and allow to cool completely, 1 to 2 hours, before unmolding. The bread pudding is best when served within 2 hours of being baked so that it does not need to be reheated.

DECOR

¼ cup powdered sugar

Whipped cream (optional)

Chocolate Sauce or Vanilla Sauce (page 169 or 170) (optional)

1. Allow the bread pudding to cool to room temperature, about 1 to 2 hours, before releasing it from the pan. When the bread pudding is cool enough to unmold, begin by pushing the bottom of the cake pan up and out of the pan. Next, slide the blade of a metal spatula or a long knife between the bread pudding and the bottom of the cake pan to separate. Cut the bread pudding into slices and slide each slice off the bottom of the cake pan and onto a serving platter, reassembling the cake in the shape of the pan.

2. Fill a small sieve with the powdered sugar and sprinkle generously over the bread pudding.

3. Serve the bread pudding with whipped cream and sauce, if desired.

Bonaparte

Pierre Hermé, the world-renowned French pastry chef, introduced me to the idea of pairing salt and chocolate at his Paris boutique on Rue Bonaparte. At his school, I was fortunate enough to take a class in which delicate French sea salt was combined with chocolate and caramel. The Bonaparte marries his techniques and my inspirations, and the result is *impeccable!*

Tuaca is a sweet, golden brown liqueur with vanilla and orange undertones, originally made in Italy and dating back to the Renaissance. If Tuaca is not available, substitute dark rum or pure vanilla extract.

CHOCOLATE SOUR CREAM CAKE

MAKES ONE 10-INCH CAKE | SERVES 14 TO 16 **(see page 151)**

TUACA SIMPLE SYRUP

½ cup granulated sugar

⅓ cup Tuaca liqueur

1. Combine the sugar with ½ cup water in a small, heavy saucepan over medium-high heat and bring to a boil, stirring occasionally. Remove from the heat, pour into a clean bowl, and allow to cool.

2. Once fully cooled, stir in the liqueur. The syrup will keep for up to 3 days in an airtight container in the refrigerator.

SEMISWEET CHOCOLATE GANACHE

(see page 85)

SALTED CHOCOLATE CHIPS

2 ounces (⅓ cup) 70% bittersweet chocolate, coarsely chopped

¼ teaspoon French sea salt (such as *sel de Guérande*)

1. Melt the chocolate in a medium, heatproof mixing bowl set over a pan of simmering water (do not allow the bowl to touch the water), stirring occasionally. Using a long offset spatula, evenly spread a thin layer of melted chocolate onto a 12-by-16-inch sheet of parchment paper. Sprinkle the salt evenly over the chocolate and cover with a second sheet of parchment. Using a rolling pin, firmly roll over the top of the paper to press the salt into the chocolate. Place in the refrigerator for 30 minutes to harden.

2. Peel off the top layer of paper from the hardened chocolate. Chop the chocolate into very small pieces, roughly half the size of a standard chocolate chip, or place the chocolate in a resealable plastic bag and hit it with the back of a spoon. Store in an airtight container in the refrigerator for up to 2 days.

SALTED CHOCOLATE CHIP MOUSSE

1½ cups heavy cream

8.5 ounces (1½ cups) 64% bittersweet chocolate, coarsely chopped

½ cup granulated sugar

2 large eggs

5 large egg yolks

1 recipe Salted Chocolate Chips

1. In the bowl of a stand mixer fitted with the whisk attachment, whip the cream until soft peaks form, 1 to 2 minutes. Hold in the refrigerator until ready to use.

2. Melt the chocolate in a medium, heatproof mixing bowl set over a pan of simmering water (do not allow the bowl to touch the water), stirring occasionally.

3. Combine the sugar with 2 tablespoons water in a small, heavy saucepan over medium-high heat and bring to a boil. Insert a candy thermometer and cook to 230° to 240°F, the soft-ball stage.

4. While the sugar is cooking, combine the whole eggs and egg yolks in the bowl of a stand mixer fitted with the whisk attachment. Whip on medium-high speed until thick and light, about 2 minutes. Carefully pour the hot sugar syrup into the whipping yolks in a continuous stream, being careful to avoid pouring the syrup directly onto the moving whisk. Increase the mixer speed to high and whip until the mixture has cooled down and has tripled in volume, 7 to 10 minutes. Reduce the mixer speed to medium and add the melted warm chocolate in several additions to ensure proper emulsification. Mix until fully combined. Remove the bowl from the mixer. Using a rubber spatula, gently fold in the whipped cream. When blended, fold in the Salted Chocolate Chips. The Salted Chocolate Chip Mousse is best made when ready to assemble the cake.

SALTED CARAMEL

1¼ cups heavy cream

½ cup glucose or light corn syrup

¾ cup granulated sugar

1 teaspoon French sea salt (such as *sel de Guérande*)

2 tablespoons unsalted butter, room temperature, cut into ¼-inch cubes

1. Bring the cream almost to a boil in a small, heavy saucepan over medium heat. Because the cream needs to be hot when incorporating it into the warm caramel, it may be necessary to hold it over very low heat once hot and until ready to use.

2. Meanwhile, combine the glucose, sugar, and salt in a medium, heavy saucepan over medium heat and boil, stirring occasionally, for approximately 4 minutes. Insert a candy thermometer and cook until the temperature reaches 310°F, about 4 minutes. The mixture should become light amber in color. Watch carefully, as caramel can go from light to burnt very quickly. Carefully mix in the butter and stir continuously until the thermometer reads 350°F. The caramel should continue to boil as you stir, and the color should darken to a deep golden brown. Very carefully pour the warm cream into the hot caramel and stir well until smooth and completely combined. *Be extremely careful when adding any liquid into a hot caramel, as the caramel may spatter.*

3. Pour the hot caramel into a clean bowl and let cool at room temperature before using. The Salted Caramel can be made up to 3 days in advance and kept in an airtight container in the refrigerator, but will need to be gently reheated until liquid and warm (but not hot) before using (see page 12).

Chocolate Sour Cream Cake, baked and cooled

1 recipe Tuaca Simple Syrup

About 2 cups Semisweet Chocolate Ganache, reheated (see page 12)

1 recipe Salted Chocolate Chip Mousse

4 tablespoons Salted Caramel, warm (see page 12)

1. Place the unwrapped cake on a flat work surface. Using a long serrated knife, slice off the top ¼ inch to even out the top of the cake as necessary. Slice the cake horizontally into 3 even layers.

2. Using a 10-inch round cake board as the bottom of a 10-by-3-inch round cake pan with removable bottom (see page 13), place 1 cake layer on the cake board, cut side up. Using a pastry brush, moisten the cake layer with one-third of the Tuaca Simple Syrup.

3. Using an offset spatula, spread ½ to ¾ cup of the Semisweet Chocolate Ganache evenly onto the syrup-soaked cake layer and cover with approximately half of the Salted Chocolate Chip Mousse. Drizzle 2 tablespoons of the Salted Caramel over the mousse.

4. Cover with a second layer of cake and repeat with another one-third of the simple syrup, ½ to ¾ cup of ganache, the remaining Salted Caramel Mousse, and the remaining 2 tablespoons Salted Caramel.

5. Top with the final layer of cake and moisten with the remaining Tuaca Simple Syrup. Spread a thin layer of Semisweet Chocolate Ganache, approximately ½ cup, as evenly and as smoothly as possible, over the top of the cake. Tightly wrap the cake in the pan in plastic wrap and place in the freezer overnight.

ALMOND PRALINE

Grapeseed or vegetable oil or unsalted butter for coating

1¼ cups granulated sugar

2 cups sliced almonds, lightly toasted and cooled

1. Lightly coat a baking sheet with oil or butter, or line the baking sheet with a Silpat and set aside.

2. Combine the sugar with ⅓ cup water in a small, heavy saucepan over medium-high heat and bring to a boil. Insert a candy thermometer and cook to 350°F, about 10 minutes. The mixture should be smooth and have darkened to a medium golden brown color. Remove the saucepan from the heat and set the candy thermometer aside. Using a wooden spoon or rubber spatula, carefully fold in the toasted almonds.

3. Using an offset spatula, evenly spread the praline onto the prepared baking sheet and set aside to cool. The Almond Praline should be made the day you will be decorating the cake. If made too far in advance, it becomes very sticky and difficult to work with.

1½ cups **Semisweet Chocolate Ganache**, reheated (see page 12)

1⅓ cups **Salted Caramel**

1 recipe **Almond Praline**

Caramel Sauce or **Chocolate Sauce** (page 168 or 169) (optional)

1. Warm the Semisweet Chocolate Ganache in a small, heavy saucepan over medium heat until melted and smooth.

2. Remove the assembled cake from the freezer, remove the plastic wrap, and unmold the cake from the pan (see page 14). Place the cake on a wire rack set over a baking sheet. Using a long metal spatula, spread the liquid ganache evenly over the top of the frozen cake. The edges and top of the cake should be very smooth and have a very finished look.

3. Place the cake in the refrigerator for about 30 minutes or until the ganache is very well set. This ganache layer needs to be solid and firm because you will be pouring the heated Salted Caramel over it and you don't want the ganache to melt. You are creating the second and final layer with the caramel, so it is important that both layers are very even and smooth.

4. Once the ganache has hardened on the cake, warm the Salted Caramel in a small, heavy saucepan over medium heat until melted and smooth.

5. Remove the ganache-covered cake from the refrigerator and place on a wire rack set over a baking sheet. Pour the heated Salted Caramel over the top of the cake and spread it evenly around the sides.

6. Place the caramel-covered cake on a doily-covered 12-inch round cake board or directly onto a cake plate. Defrost the cake in the refrigerator for 6 to 8 hours or overnight. The cake can sit at room temperature for up to 1 hour before serving.

7. When ready to serve, break up some of the Almond Praline into 1-inch shardlike pieces and use these to cover the bottom edge of the cake. Break the remaining praline into larger pieces and decoratively insert these into the center of the cake in a jagged, fanlike pattern. Use as much of this as you like, creating your own artistic touch. The cake should appear very dramatic with these pieces. Serve slices with sauce, if desired.

Vallarta

When I worked in Mexico, it was sometimes difficult to find certain ingredients needed for a specific dessert. But there were always plenty of limes and lots of tequila! Today, the smell of fresh lime reminds me of those sun-filled days, and the flavors and fragrance of this cake perfectly capture that essence.

This cake calls for a curd prepared in a nontraditional way, by cooking the eggs with the acid in the lime juice, rather than with heat. If this still makes you nervous, you can use pasteurized eggs. I use a lime sponge cake as the base, to support the rich flavors and textures of all the layers.

LIME SPONGE CAKE

MAKES ONE 10-INCH CAKE

SERVES 14 TO 16

½ cup unsalted butter, melted but not hot, plus 2 teaspoons, for greasing pan

4 large eggs

2 cups powdered sugar, sifted

½ cup whole milk

Grated zest of 2 medium limes

2 cups all-purpose flour

1 tablespoon baking powder

1. Preheat the oven to 325°F. Butter the bottom and sides of a 10-by-3-inch round cake pan with removable bottom with 2 teaspoons of the melted butter and line the bottom with a 10-inch-diameter parchment paper round.

2. In the bowl of a stand mixer fitted with the paddle attachment, beat together the eggs and powdered sugar on medium speed until light in color and thick, about 5 minutes. Slowly pour in the milk and continue mixing for 2 minutes. Pour in the remaining ½ cup melted butter and mix for another 2 minutes. Add the lime zest, being careful not to overmix the batter at this point. Remove the bowl from the mixer.

3. Sift together the flour and baking powder. Using a rubber spatula, gently fold the sifted ingredients into the batter until fully combined.

4. Pour the batter into the prepared cake pan and place on a rack in the center of the oven. Bake until the cake is golden brown, 50 to 55 minutes.

5. Remove the cake from the oven and allow to cool completely. Once cooled, remove the cake from the pan (see page 12) and peel the parchment paper from the bottom of the cake. Wrap the cake tightly in plastic wrap until ready to use. The Lime Sponge Cake can be stored for up to 1 day in the refrigerator or in the freezer for up to 1 week.

LIME CURD

2 (14-ounce) cans sweetened condensed milk

6 large egg yolks

Grated zest of 4 medium limes

1 cup freshly squeezed lime juice, strained

Using a hand whisk, combine all the ingredients in a nonreactive mixing bowl and whisk until blended. Cover tightly with plastic wrap and refrigerate overnight. The Lime Curd can be prepared up to 1 day in advance; 1¼ cups will be used in the Lime Pastry Cream, ¾ cup in the Lime Whipped Cream, ½ cup will be used for Decor, and the remaining 1 cup will be used to assemble the cake.

TEQUILA SIMPLE SYRUP

½ cup granulated sugar

¼ cup silver tequila

3 tablespoons freshly squeezed lime juice, strained

1. Combine the sugar with ½ cup water in a small, heavy saucepan over medium-high heat and bring to a boil, stirring occasionally. Remove from the heat, pour into a clean bowl, and allow to cool.

2. Once fully cooled, stir in the tequila and lime juice until combined. The Tequila Simple Syrup will keep for up to 1 day in an airtight container in the refrigerator.

LIME PASTRY CREAM

2 cups heavy cream

¾ cup whole milk

½ vanilla bean, scraped (see page 12)

⅓ cup granulated sugar

4 large egg yolks

1 tablespoon cornstarch

1 tablespoon potato starch

¼ cup plus 1 tablespoon unsalted butter, room temperature

3 gelatin sheets (see page 11)

1¼ cups Lime Curd

1. Combine 1 cup cream, the milk, and vanilla bean seeds in a medium, heavy saucepan over medium-high heat and bring to a boil.

2. In a mixing bowl, whisk together the sugar, egg yolks, and both starches until well combined and smooth. While whisking continuously, slowly pour the warm cream mixture over the egg mixture and whisk until well incorporated. Return all to the saucepan and continue to cook over medium heat, whisking continuously, until the mixture begins to boil and has thickened to the consistency of a loose pudding. Strain through a fine-mesh sieve into a clean mixing bowl and stir in 1 tablespoon butter until fully combined and smooth. Cover with plastic wrap, pressing directly onto the surface of the custard. Cool in the refrigerator for 1 hour.

3. Once the custard has cooled and is ready to use, remove from the refrigerator.

4. In the bowl of a stand mixer fitted with the whisk attachment, whip the remaining 1 cup cream until soft peaks form, about 1 minute. Hold in the refrigerator until ready to use.

5. Soften the gelatin sheets in 3 cups cool water for 5 minutes. Squeeze out the excess water, then melt the gelatin in a small saucepan over low heat until liquid.

6. In the bowl of a stand mixer fitted with either the whisk or the paddle attachment, lightly beat the cooled pastry cream just to loosen. Add ¼ cup butter and mix until combined. While the machine is running, pour in the melted gelatin and mix until fully dissolved and smooth. Remove the bowl from the mixer. Using a rubber spatula, gently fold in the whipped cream until just combined, then fold in the Lime Curd. Because it contains gelatin, the Lime Pastry Cream should be made when you are ready to assemble the cake.

LIME WHIPPED CREAM

3 cups heavy cream

¼ cup granulated sugar

¾ cup Lime Curd

1. In the bowl of a stand mixer fitted with the whisk attachment, whip together the cream and sugar until stiff peaks form, 2 to 3 minutes. Remove the bowl from the mixer. Using a rubber spatula, fold in the Lime Curd until combined.

2. Fit a pastry bag with a ½-inch, plain, round decorating tip and fill with half of Lime Whipped Cream. Hold all in the refrigerator until ready to use. The Lime Whipped Cream must be used within 15 minutes of preparation.

ASSEMBLY

Lime Sponge Cake, baked
and cooled

1 recipe Tequila Simple Syrup

1 recipe Lime Pastry Cream

1 cup Lime Curd

1 recipe Lime Whipped Cream

1. Place the unwrapped cake on a flat work surface. Using a long serrated knife, slice off the top ¼ inch to even out the top of the cake as necessary. Slice the cake horizontally into 3 even layers.

2. Using a 10-inch round cake board as the bottom of a 10-by-3-inch round cake pan with removable bottom (see page 13), place 1 cake layer on the cake board, cut side up. Using a pastry brush, moisten the cake layer with one-third of the Tequila Simple Syrup.

3. Measure out ½ cup of the Lime Pastry Cream and set aside to be used on the top layer of the cake. Using an offset spatula, spread half of the remaining Lime Pastry Cream evenly onto the syrup-soaked cake layer and top with ½ cup of Lime Curd. Using the prepared pastry bag, pipe a layer of Lime Whipped Cream over the Lime Curd in a spiral pattern, using the entire bag. Refill the bag with the remaining Lime Whipped Cream to be used on the next layer.

4. Top with a second layer of cake and repeat with another one-third of the simple syrup, the remaining ½ cup Lime Pastry Cream, and the rest of the Lime Curd. Finish with piped Lime Whipped Cream.

5. Top with the final layer of cake, moisten with the remaining Tequila Simple Syrup, and cover with the reserved ½ cup of Lime Pastry Cream. Tightly wrap the cake in the pan in plastic wrap and place in the freezer overnight.

DECOR

2 cups large unsweetened
coconut chips

1½ cups heavy cream

1½ tablespoons granulated
sugar

½ cup Lime Curd

¼ cup powdered sugar

Strawberry Sauce (page 170)
(optional)

1. Preheat the oven to 300°F. Spread the coconut chips on a baking sheet and toast in the oven until slightly colored, 5 to 7 minutes. Set aside to cool.

2. In the bowl of a stand mixer fitted with the whisk attachment, whip together the cream and granulated sugar until stiff peaks form, 1 to 2 minutes. Fold the Lime Curd into the whipped cream.

3. Remove the assembled cake from the freezer, remove the plastic wrap, and unmold the cake from the pan (see page 14). Using an offset spatula, spread a thick layer of Lime Whipped Cream around the sides and top of the cake as evenly as possible, using up all of the whipped cream. Press the toasted coconut evenly around the sides of the cake (see page 14) to completely cover the whipped cream. Sprinkle any remaining coconut over the top of the cake. Place the decorated cake in the refrigerator to defrost for 8 hours.

4. When ready to serve, fill a small sieve with the powdered sugar and generously dust the top of the cake. Place the cake on a doily-covered, 12-inch round cake board or directly onto a cake plate. The cake is best served cold but can sit at room temperature for up to 1 hour before serving. Serve slices with sauce, if desired.

Sauces

As a French-trained pastry chef, I serve my desserts with sauces to enhance flavors and create a beautiful presentation when plating each slice or piece. When entertaining at home, a sauce that perfectly complements your cake truly is worth the extra effort. However, the use of these sauces is purely optional. I include my favorite pairing suggestions, but by all means create your own extraordinary combinations.

To serve, simply drizzle a tablespoon of sauce onto one side of each individual plate and place a slice of cake alongside. If you're in an adventurous mood, put two different sauces in separate squeeze bottles and paint a pretty pattern on the plate. Most important, have fun trying as few or as many sauces as you wish.

The following recipes each yield 1 cup of sauce.

BLACKBERRY SAUCE

3 cups frozen blackberries (no sugar added), thawed

3 tablespoons granulated sugar

Combine the berries and sugar in a food processor or blender and blend until smooth. Strain through a fine-mesh sieve into a clean bowl. Cover and chill in the refrigerator until ready to use. Blackberry Sauce can be made up to 2 days in advance.

Serve alongside the following cakes:
Blackberry Cheesecake, page 124   *Lemon Praline Torte*,
Citronesse, page 94   page 20
Ivoire Royale, page 34   *Lemon Ricotta*, page 74
                                       Marco Polo, page 50

CARAMEL SAUCE

2 large egg yolks

1 tablespoon plus ½ cup granulated sugar

¼ cup whole milk

2 tablespoons plus ⅓ cup heavy cream

1 vanilla bean, scraped (see page 12)

1. In a heatproof mixing bowl, whisk together the egg yolks and 1 tablespoon of sugar until frothy.

2. Combine the milk, 2 tablespoons cream, and the vanilla bean seeds in a medium, heavy saucepan over medium-high heat and bring almost to a boil. While whisking continuously, slowly pour the warm milk over the yolk-sugar mixture and whisk until blended. Return all to the saucepan and cook over medium heat, stirring continuously with a rubber spatula, until the mixture thickens to a very loose custard, approximately 1 minute. Strain through a fine-mesh sieve into a clean bowl and allow to cool slightly at room temperature.

3. Place the remaining ½ cup sugar in a small, heavy saucepan over medium-high heat and cook the sugar until it begins to caramelize and turn an amber color, about 4 minutes. Remove the pan from the heat and slowly and carefully mix in the warm vanilla custard. Once all of the custard has been added, return the pan to the heat and cook, stirring continuously, until all of the caramel has dissolved into the custard and the mixture is completely smooth.

4. Warm up the remaining ⅓ cup cream in the microwave or on the stovetop until hot and pour into the sauce, mixing until smooth. Allow to cool, cover, and chill in the refrigerator until ready to use. Caramel Sauce can be made up to 2 days in advance. Reheat gently on the stovetop until liquid before using (see page 13).

Serve alongside the following cakes:
Banana Cream Torte, page 112
Bonaparte, page 159
New York, New York, page 108
Versailles, page 134
Viking, page 42

CHOCOLATE SAUCE

⅓ cup cocoa powder

½ cup granulated sugar

¼ cup heavy cream

1. Sift the cocoa powder into a small bowl. Add the sugar and mix until combined.

2. Combine the cream with ⅓ cup plus 1 tablespoon water in a small, heavy saucepan over medium-high heat and bring to a boil. Gradually stir in the cocoa powder and sugar. Return to a boil, stirring continuously until the sauce appears to bubble and begins to thicken. Strain into a clean bowl. Cover and chill in the refrigerator until ready to use. Chocolate Sauce can be made up to 3 days in advance.

Serve alongside the following cakes:
Amor Chocolat, page 151
Bonaparte, page 159
Chocolate Nirvana, page 71
Dame Chocolat, page 31
Diamond Head, page 67
Holiday Yule Log, page 139
Love Is Chocolate, page 157
New York, New York, page 108
Tortamisù, page 120
Viking, page 42

KIWI SAUCE

4 ripe, medium kiwi fruit, peeled

¼ cup granulated sugar

4 teaspoons freshly squeezed lemon juice

Slice each kiwi fruit into 6 pieces and place in the bowl of a food processor. Add the sugar and lemon juice and puree until very smooth. Pour into a clean bowl (do not strain). Cover and chill in the refrigerator until ready to use. This sauce should be made the day it is being served. Otherwise, it may discolor and the flavor will not be as fresh.

Serve alongside the following cakes:
Lemon Praline Torte, page 21
Passion Fruit Ricotta Cake, page 57

MANGO SAUCE

1 cup diced, peeled, pitted mango
(from 1 large ripe mango)

1 tablespoon freshly squeezed lemon juice

¼ cup granulated sugar

Combine the mango, lemon juice, and sugar in the bowl of a food processor and blend until smooth. Add 2 tablespoons water and pulse to combine. The sauce should become thinner. Add more water by tablespoonfuls as necessary until it reaches the desired consistency. The sauce should be fairly thick but pourable. Cover and chill in the refrigerator until ready to use. Mango Sauce is best made on the day you are serving it.

Serve alongside the following cakes:
Blood Orange Ricotta Cake, page 129
Bora Bora, page 89
Caribe, page 83
Chocolate Nirvana, page 71
Lemon Praline Torte, page 21

PASSION FRUIT SAUCE

½ cup frozen passion fruit puree, thawed

1 small ripe banana, cut into chunks

¼ cup granulated sugar

Combine all the ingredients in the bowl of a food processor and puree until smooth. Strain through a fine-mesh sieve into a clean bowl. Cover and chill in the refrigerator until ready to use. Passion Fruit Sauce may be made up to 2 days in advance.

Serve alongside the following cakes:
Banana Cream Torte, page 113
Caribe, page 83
Passion Fruit Ricotta Cake, page 57

RASPBERRY SAUCE

3 cups frozen raspberries (no sugar added), thawed

3 tablespoons granulated sugar

Combine the raspberries and sugar in a food processor or blender and puree until smooth. Strain through a fine-mesh sieve into a clean bowl. Cover and chill in the refrigerator until ready to use. Raspberry Sauce may be made up to 2 days in advance.

Serve alongside the following cakes:
Beau Soleil, page 60
Blood Orange Ricotta Cake, page 129
Chocolate Nirvana, page 71
Citronesse, page 94
Devika, page 39
Ivoire Royale, page 34
Lemon Praline Torte, page 21
Rasbperry White Chocolate Linzer Torte, page 145

STRAWBERRY SAUCE

5 large ripe strawberries, hulled

1 vanilla bean, scraped (see page 12)

2 tablespoons granulated sugar

1. Using a sharp paring knife, dice the strawberries into ⅛-inch cubes.

2. Combine the diced strawberries, vanilla bean seeds, and sugar in a microwave-safe bowl and cover the bowl tightly with plastic wrap. Microwave on high power for 50 seconds. Remove from the microwave and let cool at room temperature, stirring if needed to combine. This recipe yields a chunky sauce with lots of texture and flavor. Cover and chill in the refrigerator until ready to use. Strawberry Sauce is best when made 1 to 2 days in advance.

Serve alongside the following cakes:
Lemon Praline Torte, page 21
Strawberry Poppy Seed Cake, page 98
Strawberry Shortcakes, page 80
Vallarta, page 165

TROPICAL FRUIT SAUCE

½ large ripe banana, cut into ¼-inch cubes

½ cup diced, peeled, pitted mango (from 1 small ripe mango), cut into ⅛-inch cubes

¼ cup frozen passion fruit puree, thawed

1½ tablespoons granulated sugar

In a small mixing bowl, gently stir the chopped fruit into the juice until combined. Cover and chill in the refrigerator until ready to use. Tropical Fruit Sauce is best when made 1 day before serving.

Serve alongside the following cakes:
Beau Soleil, page 60
Bora Bora, page 89

VANILLA SAUCE

3 large egg yolks

2 tablespoons granulated sugar

½ cup whole milk

¼ cup plus 1 tablespoon heavy cream

1 vanilla bean, scraped (see page 12)

1. In a heatproof, nonreactive mixing bowl, whisk together the egg yolks and sugar until frothy.

2. Combine the milk, cream, and vanilla bean seeds in a medium, heavy saucepan over medium-high heat and bring almost to a boil. While whisking continuously, slowly pour the warm cream over the eggs and sugar and whisk until blended. Return all to the saucepan and cook over medium heat, stirring continuously with a rubber spatula, until the mixture thickens to a very loose custard, 1 to 2 minutes. Strain through a fine-mesh sieve into a clean bowl and allow to cool at room temperature. Cover and chill in the refrigerator until ready to use. Vanilla Sauce can be made up to 1 day in advance.

Serve alongside the following cakes:
Banana Cream Torte, page 113
Beau Soleil, page 60
Dame Chocolat, page 30
Diamond Head, page 67
Holiday Yule Log, page 139
Love Is Chocolate, page 157
Marco Polo, page 50
Strawberry Poppy Seed Cake, page 98
Tortamisù, page 120
Versailles, page 135

Sources

AMAZON.COM
866-216-1072
www.amazon.com
100 percent pure yuzu juice, frozen passion fruit puree, frozen coconut puree, frozen blood orange concentrate

ATECO
800-645-7170
www.atecousa.com
Large inventory of Ateco products, including pastry tools, cutter sets, and decorating equipment

BLOOMINGDALES
800-777-0000
www.bloomingdales.com
Cookware, bakeware, and cutlery in addition to a large assortment of designer cake plates, trays, and servingware

BLUE BOTTLE COFFEE
510-653-3394
www.bluebottlecoffee.net
Exceptionally fresh roasted coffee and espresso beans, which are organic, pesticide free, and shadegrown

BOB'S RED MILL
800-553-2258
www.bobsredmill.com
Organic, whole-grain, nut, and gluten-free flours; dried fruit; coconut; sea salt; and turbinado sugar (evaporated cane juice)

CHEF RUBBER
702-614-9350
www.chefrubber.com
Unique selection of metal molds, freeze-dried fruits, novelty decorating ingredients, and finishing touches

EARTH BALANCE NATURAL
201-421-3970
www.earthbalancenatural.com
Vegan Buttery Sticks

EXTRAORDINARY DESSERTS
619-294-7001
www.extraordinarydesserts.com
Mariage Frères's Marco Polo tea, Valrhona baking chocolates and cocoa powder, dark-chocolate-covered coffee beans, cake decorating supplies

FANCY FLOURS
406-587-0118
www.fancyflours.com
A wide variety of creative baking and decorating supplies for cakes and cupcakes

FRONTIER NATURAL PRODUCTS CO-OP
800-669-3275
www.frontiercoop.com
Organic poppy seeds and spices as well as many herbs and teas

J.B. PRINCE
800-473-0577
www.jbprince.com
Large selection of high-quality imported and domestic chef's equipment, decorative molds, and specialty bakeware

KAISER BAKEWARE
800-966-3009
www.kaiserbakeware.com
Springform, Bundt, and baking pans in many shapes and sizes

KALUSTYAN'S
800-352-3451
www.kalustyans.com
Rose syrup, dried fruits and nuts, vanilla beans, flavor extracts, turbinado sugar, gelatin sheets, brown rice flour, potato starch, gluten-free all-purpose baking flour

KEREKES
800-525-5556
www.bakedeco.com
Flexible silicone bakeware, cupcake wrappers, disposable paper baking molds, cake pans, and cake boards

KING ARTHUR FLOUR BAKER'S CATALOGUE
800-827-6836
www.kingarthurflour.com / bakerscaatalogue.com
Large inventory of grain and nut flours, all kinds of gourmet decorating ingredients including chocolate pailletes as well as a large selection of appliances, bakeware, and gadgets.

KITCHENAID
800-334-6889
www.kitchenaid.com
Mixers, blenders, and food processors

L'EPICERIE
866-350-7575
www.lepicerie.com
Trablit coffee extract, frozen fruit purees, French sea salt

NEIMAN MARCUS
888-888-4757
www.neimanmarcus.com
Linens, cake plates, tea service, and table-top accessories for special occasions

NY CAKE
877-692-2538
www.nycake.com
Baking ingredients, baking equipment, tools and gadgets, long-stem birthday candles

PASTRY CHEF CENTRAL
561-999-9483
www.pastrychef.com
Edible gold and silver leaf and a large selection of imported and domestic gourmet baking ingredients including chocolate shavings and rolled chocolate "cigarettes." Also all types of specialty decorating tools and baking equipment such as scales, timers, and thermometers.

PAULETTE MACARONS
310-275-0023 / 415-864-2400
www.paulettemacarons.com
Caramel macarons

THE PERFECT PURÉE
707-261-5100
www.perfectpuree.com
Frozen fruit purees and concentrates

SUNSPIRE NATURAL CHOCOLATES
866-972-6879
www.sunspire.com
Dairy-free chocolate chips

SUR LA TABLE
800-243-0852
www.surlatable.com
High-quality stainless-steel cookware, bakeware, servingware, utensils, and Silpats

SWEETFIELDS
877-987-9338
www.sweetfields.com
Crystalized roses, petals, and other flowers

TARGET
800-591-3869
www.target.com
Large selection of bakeware, cookware, tools, appliances, and gadgets

WILLIAMS-SONOMA
877-812-6235
www.williams-sonoma.com
Large selection of high-quality chef's equipment, utensils, bakeware, and servingware

WILTON
800-794-5866
www.wilton.com
Cake decorating tips and tools, corrugated cardboard rounds, cake boxes, dowel rods, cake turntables, doilies

I would not have become a baker today if it were not for my grandma, Clara, and her sisters. Growing up, I would watch them bake and create such delicious desserts. It is a memory I treasure from my earliest days.

My mother, Sally, gifted me with the passion to bake, the desire to be creative, the drive to entertain others, and the tenacity to achieve my dreams.

Sahara, my daughter, brings me more joy than anything I have ever created.

I am grateful that my father, Jerry, let me use his home kitchen for months and months of commercial baking when I got started. This was truly the beginning of Extraordinary Desserts, and without his generosity my stores would not have been possible. My dad's wife, Martha, who has become like a mother to me, provided enthusiastic support and many hours in her kitchen testing recipes for this book.

Without my husband, Jamie Kiskis, involved as co-pilot, this book could never have taken off. Night after night he waited up late to transcribe my creations and the many edits from testing. I am thankful for this showing of love and generosity. He shared in the task of creating this book as if it were his own.

Christina Wright has been my friend and dinner buddy in New York for many years. I am fortunate that she became co-author. Without her book-writing experience, baking background, patience, and advice, this book would not be a reality.

I am so thankful that my dear friend Andre Jackson, of Jack Price Design, believed in this book enough to bless it with his creativity, elegance, and gorgeous floral touches. He nurtured me throughout the photo shoot preparation process with his thoughtfulness and good humor.

I was so fortunate to have the assistance of Gail Baral to help style many of the photos. She offered her gorgeous sense of design, impeccable attention to detail, culinary creativity, and most of all, friendship.

Lorena Nelson of Red Coral Public Relations has been my tireless public relations and marketing agent with this project and so many others. She also diligently helped coordinate the making of the book. I can never thank her enough for her dedication to my business and for our special friendship.

I am so touched that Christopher Steighner, our editor, saw something that sparkled in my book concept, and I am grateful for his belief, guidance, and support throughout the entire process.

A big thank you goes to Ray Kachatorian for making my desserts so extraordinarily beautiful through his photography, and to his assistant Tuan Tran for his helpful hands.

Thank you Andrew Whitcomb, for making sure Sahara and I were styled in case the camera was near.

Special thanks to David Nelson, a true master wordsmith, for lending his talented pen to the pages of this book.

Thank you, Lilly Ghahremani, of Full Circle Literary, for the push to get the book proposal moving in the right direction.

Thank you to Monica Parcell, our copy editor, for your attention to detail, and to Lynne Yeamans, our designer, for your artistic touch.

Thank you to Chris Casagrande for overseeing the budget and making sure we came in "sorta" close.

For allowing us to photograph on their properties, I would like to thank Patricia Applegate, Bud and Esther Fischer, and the Save Our Heritage Organization (SOHO) in San Diego, which manages the Marston House. We also appreciate Roost, L'Objet, and TableArt for lending their wonderful products for our photo shoots.

I am so grateful to my kitchen staff for going above and beyond the needs of the restaurants' kitchens to prepare the recipes, help at photo shoots, and provide delicious meals that kept us going. The cakes and savory creations are extraordinary at our restaurants because of the tireless work of the women in my kitchens. Their dedication to baking, decorating, displaying, and creating is inspiring and I appreciate them every day.

Thank you to my dedicated and talented management team and front-of-house staff, who nurture our clients every day and uphold the mission of my company. Without their support, I would not have been able to take on this project.

Thank you for testing my recipes: Kendra Altomare, Gail Baral, Tricia Campanella, Jon Cieslak, Kathleen Felt, Judee Feinberg, Wendy Gamboa, Patty Gladstone, Angela Goding, Betty Ervin, Jill and Lindsay Koenig, Jordan Krant, Martha Krasne, Julia Long, Erin McKay, Judy Miller, Cathleen Price, Rachel Pauta, Christopher Steighner, Johanna Steinberg, and Christina Wright.

To our loyal Extraordinary Desserts customers from San Diego and beyond, thank you for enjoying our desserts and supporting our passion for more than twenty-two years. Your continued patronage and unwavering enthusiasm have allowed Extraordinary Desserts to flourish into what it is today and ultimately made this book possible. Our fans are our greatest source of inspiration and encouragement.